Microsoft Azure: Enterprise Application Development

Straight talking advice on how to design and build enterprise applications for the cloud

Richard J. Dudley

Nathan A. Duchene

[PACKT] enterprise
PUBLISHING
professional expertise distilled

BIRMINGHAM - MUMBAI

Microsoft Azure: Enterprise Application Development

First published: December 2010

Production Reference: 1231110

Published by Packt Publishing Ltd.
32 Lincoln Road
Olton
Birmingham, B27 6PA, UK.

ISBN 978-1-849680-98-1

www.packtpub.com

Cover Image by Vinayak Chittar (vinayak.chittar@gmail.com)

Credits

Authors
Richard J. Dudley

Nathan A. Duchene

Reviewers
Ruslan Konviser

Anton Staykov

Acquisition Editor
James Lumsden

Development Editor
Dhwani Devater

Technical Editor
Gaurav Datar

Indexer
Rekha Nair

Editorial Team Leader
Gagandeep Singh

Project Team Leader
Lata Basantani

Project Coordinator
Rebecca Sawant

Proofreader
Ting Baker

Graphics
Geetanjali Sawant

Production Coordinator
Shantanu Zagade

Cover Work
Shantanu Zagade

About the Authors

Richard J. Dudley has experience in the field of computers, going all way back to PC-DOS 1.1 (of which the original box still sits in a closet), with 128K and dual floppies. He began programming in GW-BASIC, and has used nearly every BASIC variant along the way. He was very active in the Louisville BBS community in the 1980s.

Richard holds a BS in Environmental Science from Allegheny College, and an MS in Biological Sciences from The University of Alabama. He developed his programming skills as a way to record and analyze his data, and later collaborate with other labs as the World Wide Web slowly came into being. Eventually, the dot com boom was too tempting, and Rich left science to be become a full-time developer. Rich spent 10 years as an Enterprise Developer, building and supporting everything from consumer websites to several mission-critical systems integrations, to Crystal-and SSRS-based BI tools, to a number of internal line-of-business applications.

Rich is now a Technology Evangelist for ComponentOne, where his job is to support the user community by working with all the latest Microsoft technologies.

Rich's past employers include The University of Alabama-Birmingham (Research Assistant V), The University of Pittsburgh (Research Specialist II), Spang & Co. (e-Commerce Developer), and Armada Supply Chain Solutions (Senior Application Developer).

Acknowledgement

You always see an author thank his or her family, and until you write a book, you can't really understand why. Writing a book is time consuming—you spend a lot of time looking out of a window watching the seasons pass by, wishing you were kayaking on the nearby lake, or going for a bike ride, or anything other than being inside staring at a glowing rectangle hoping the words start flowing soon. We've made almost one complete turn around the sun since we started this book, and it is the culmination of a great deal of work.

So, at the risk of sounding clichéd, I have to thank my wife Kathy, and daughter Anna Claire, who can now have her daddy back.

The impetus to write a technical book doesn't come from money—there's a small advance, and if you're really lucky, maybe some royalties. Fame? Not really—if you're popular, maybe a dozen people will tweet about you. The urge to write a book comes from something more fundamental, something our parents instilled in us and we try and instill in our children—sharing. Share your experiences, share what you know, as doing so builds a stronger community. I hope you find what we've done to be useful.

Nathan A. Duchene has been developing in the .NET Framework since 2005, starting with ASP.NET 2.0. He found a need for a website with the features available in ASP.NET, and with some guidance from Richard J. Dudley, quickly developed and published his web application to the world. After experiencing the ease and flexibility offered by .NET to developers, he decided to learn more features, best practices, and tricks to enhance his web application, build new web applications, write and maintain some console applications, and much more.

In 2008, Nathan and Richard developed and entered a web application into a coding contest, which was voted by the community as the second best of all submissions, losing only by a few votes. Winning an MSDN Premium subscription, it allowed Nathan to play with a number of systems and tools, strengthening his knowledge in the development world.

Nathan, along with Richard, was part of a group that gave a presentation on Silverlight 2 in the Windows Azure cloud in 2009. Both technologies were in beta or pre-beta phases, which caused unexpected issues. Even though the application would not work, the talk was a great success in explaining Windows Azure and Silverlight 2 before they were released to the world.

Nathan is currently an Application Developer for a supply chain solutions company based in Pittsburgh, PA. Along with some .NET development, he also develops and administers solutions using Microsoft SQL Server 2000/2005/2008, Microsoft Biztalk Server 2009, and Microsoft Office SharePoint Server 2007.

This is Nathan's first book and has been a tremendous experience from front to back. After being given the opportunity to pass on some knowledge back to the community, he hopes to have the opportunity in the future to write more books for the community. After observing how quickly technology changes, he feels it's important to release up-to-date information for others to make use of. While Nathan and Richard had to re-write numerous chapters along the way to include new features or changes to existing features, the experience was amazing.

Acknowledgement

I'd like to thank my family and friends for all the support throughout the book process. Not only did they support me, but the encouragement helped me through some rough times when I thought it to be a difficult task to be physically able to write the book with everything else going on at the time. Without my friends and family, I couldn't have made it through this journey. Most importantly, I'd also like to thank my co-author, Richard Dudley. He has been a colleague, a friend, and a mentor over the last eight years. He's shown me opportunities that no one else has and I'm really happy to have him around as a partner in everything we've done. Richard's enthusiasm to help me flourish personally and professionally has had the most meaning in my life recently, and I look forward to working side-by-side with him over the next decades.

About the Reviewer

Anton Staykov has over nine years of solid experience in developing dynamic software solutions (corporate web portals, rich media sites, e-commerce sites, internal software solutions covering specific business needs), using the latest technologies, including Microsoft .NET, MS SQL Server, PHP, MySQL. Currently he is Technical Evangelist for a world leader in the field of User Interface Development Tools and User Experience services. He is User Group Lead for Windows Azure User Group Bulgaria. Anton is an Engineer in Telecommunications and Master of Science in Internet Software Technologies.

You can visit his blog at: `http://blogs.staykov.net/`.

Table of Contents

Preface	**1**
Chapter 1: Introduction to Cloud Computing	**7**
What is an enterprise application?	7
What is cloud computing?	8
Some benefits of cloud computing	9
Some downsides of cloud computing	10
Cloud computing infrastructure	11
Cloudy skies ahead	12
Is cloud computing "enterprisey" enough?	13
Summary	14
Chapter 2: The Nickel Tour of Azure	**15**
Explaining Azure to the managers	15
Windows Azure	17
Compute service	17
Storage service	18
Blob Storage	18
Table Storage	19
Queue Storage	19
Azure Fabric Agent and Controller	20
SQL Azure	20
Windows Azure platform: AppFabric	21
Codename Dallas	22
Development Fabric	22
Considerations for the ASP.NET developer	22
How are Azure costs calculated?	23
Calculating Windows Azure pricing	23

Calculating SQL Azure pricing	24
Calculating AppFabric pricing	24
Summary	**25**
Chapter 3: Setting Up for Development	**27**
Downloading the tools	**27**
Configuring the local machine for development	**27**
Installing Windows Azure tools and SDK	**31**
Summary	**34**
Chapter 4: Designing our Sample Application	**35**
Project design	**35**
Integrating application with cloud features	**37**
Creating an Azure account	**39**
Summary	**40**
Chapter 5: Introduction to SQL Azure	**41**
Overview of SQL Azure	**41**
Manageability	43
Managing SQL Azure	43
High availability	45
Scalability	46
Relational data model	46
Familiar development model	46
What's the same in SQL Azure?	47
Data types	47
Database objects	47
Fully supported T-SQL commands	48
Partially supported T-SQL commands	49
SQL Server built-in functions	49
Multiple active result sets	50
What's different in SQL Azure?	50
Number of databases	51
Database objects	51
Service Broker, SQL Browser, and DTC	51
T-SQL commands	51
System functions	52
Data synchronization	52
Security	**53**
Development considerations	**54**
Managing maximum size	54
Management tools	**55**
SQL Azure portal	55
SSMS 2008 R2	55
Project Houston	55

Access 2010	56
Managing databases, logins, and roles in SQL Azure	**56**
Migrating schema and data	**57**
Manually scripting objects and data	57
SQL Azure Migration Wizard	58
SQL Server Integration Services (SSIS)	59
SQL Server Import and Export Wizard	59
Creating packages from scratch	61
DAC Packs	61
BCP	62
The Jupiter Motor's ERP system database and the Dealer Orders database	**62**
SQL Azure portal	64
Creating our database	**65**
Summary	**76**

Chapter 6: Azure Blob Storage	**77**
Blobs in the Azure ecosystem	**77**
Creating Blob Storage	**78**
Windows Azure Content Delivery Network	**82**
Blob Storage Data Model	**83**
Blob Storage	**83**
Representational State Transfer	84
The Blob Storage API	84
Working with containers using the REST interface	84
Working with containers using the StorageClient library	85
Working with blobs	88
Summary	**91**

Chapter 7: Azure Table Storage	**93**
Table Storage versus database tables	**93**
Some of the good stuff	**95**
Limitations of Table Storage	**96**
Adding Table Storage to an Azure account	**96**
Accessing Table Storage	**97**
Working with tables	98
Working with entities	99
Entity Group Transactions	103
Choosing a PartitionKey	**103**
Exception handling	**104**
Retry on exceptions	104
Exceptions on retry	105
Concurrency conflicts	105

Table errors and HTTP response codes	105
Summary	**105**
Chapter 8: Queue Storage	**107**
The ins and outs of queues	**107**
Reasons to use a queue	109
Invisibility time and failover	109
Special handling for binary data	110
Working with queues	**110**
Listing queues	111
REST API	111
Client library	112
Creating queues	112
REST API	112
Client library	113
Deleting queues	113
REST API	113
Client library	113
Setting metadata	113
REST API	113
Client library	114
Getting metadata	114
REST API	114
Client library	114
Working with messages	**114**
Summary	**117**
Chapter 9: Web Role	**119**
The role of the web	**119**
Web roles, déjà vu, and ASP.NET	**120**
Creating the solution and web role project	121
Application diagnostics and logging in the cloud	**123**
Jupiter Motors web role	**126**
How do we get there? Here's our code!	128
Additional stored procedures used by the web role	128
Summary	**142**
Chapter 10: Web Services and Azure	**143**
Web services and WCF	**143**
Securing WCF	**144**
Jupiter Motors web service	**145**
Creating a new WCF service web role	**145**
Our WCF web services	**149**
ERP service interface—IERPService.vb	149
Service Contract	150

Operation Contract 150
Data Contract 150
Using ADO.NET datasets 151
ERP service implementation—ERPService.svc.vb 151
LoadStartupData service function 152
GetOrderStatusForOrder service function 152
AddOrderStatusUpdateToQueue service function 153
GetOrdersNotComplete, GetOrderStatuses, and
CreateDataSetFromDataReader class functions 153

DataTable "gotcha" **155**
Web Service Definition Language (WSDL) "gotcha" **156**
Summary **157**

Chapter 11: Worker Roles **159**
Worker role internals **159**
Uses of worker roles **160**
Externally facing worker roles 161
Thread-pool pattern 161
Managing worker roles **161**
Best practices 162
The Jupiter Motors worker role **163**
Building the Jupiter Motors worker role 163
Summary **168**

Chapter 12: Local Application for Updates **169**
Brief overview of the application **169**
JupiterMotorsERP local application **170**
Adding App.config code 173
Testing our application **175**
Summary **176**

Chapter 13: Azure AppFabric **177**
Introduction to Azure AppFabric **177**
Access Control **178**
Authentication versus authorization 180
Basics of Access Control configuration 181
Requests and Simple Web Tokens 182
Configuring Access Control for Jupiter Motors 183
Configuring Azure AppFabric Portal 184
Configuration tools 186
Creating a Token Policy 188
Configuring a Scope 190
Configuring an Issuer 190
Configuring a Rule 190
Configuring a client application for Access Control 191
Using Access Control in a web service 194

Service Bus	**195**
Service Bus as message relay	196
Service Bus as connection broker	197
Summary	**197**
Chapter 14: Azure Monitoring and Diagnostics	**199**
Azure Diagnostics—under the hood	**200**
Enabling diagnostic logging	**202**
Changing the location of the logging configuration	204
Logging config data in our application	**206**
Transferring and persisting diagnostic data	**206**
Accessing stored data	**208**
Summary	**208**
Chapter 15: Deploying to Windows Azure	**209**
Setting up hosted service in Windows Azure	**209**
Setting Hosted Service identifiers	211
Affinity Groups—geographically grouping services	212
Preparation application for deployment	**213**
Ready for deployment	**215**
Changing live configuration	**218**
Upgrading the deployment	**219**
Running the deployment	**220**
Summary	**221**
Conclusion	**221**
Index	**223**

Preface

Microsoft's Azure platform is an exciting offering in the cloud services market space. Designed to compete with Google AppEngine and Amazon Web Services, Azure stresses a familiar development environment (primarily .NET, SQL Server, and Visual Studio) with a rich set of capabilities. In addition to using Windows Azure to host web applications and services, SQL Azure provides a relational database in the cloud, and Access Control can be utilized to integrate user accounts with identity providers. We can leverage our skills to build powerful applications on Azure with relative ease.

The aim of this book is to gain an understanding of the process, advantages, and challenges of building an application on Azure. We do this by providing in-depth discussion of the platform as we build a sample application.

What this book covers

Chapter 1, Introduction to Cloud Computing, provides an introduction to cloud computing and enterprise applications.

Chapter 2, The Nickel Tour of Azure, is an overview of the service offerings in the Microsoft Azure Platform.

Chapter 3, Setting Up for Development, shows us the tools required for developing applications for Azure and how to set up our development environments.

Chapter 4, Designing our Sample Application, provides the overview of the sample application that will be built throughout the rest of this book.

Chapter 5, Introduction to SQL Azure, provides an introduction to SQL Azure and discusses the differences between SQL Azure and SQL Server 2008. We also create the database objects for our sample application in this chapter.

Chapter 6, Azure Blob Storage, discusses the Blob Storage service and how to interact with blobs using either a .NET client library or REST services. We also create the containers and blobs for our sample application in this chapter.

Chapter 7, Azure Table Storage, discusses the Table Storage service and how to interact with tables using either a .NET client library or REST services.

Chapter 8, Queue Storage, speaks about the Queue Storage service and how to interact with queues using either a .NET client library or REST services. We also create the queues needed for our application in this chapter.

Chapter 9, Web Role, gives an overview of what a web role is, and some of the similarities and differences between a web role and a traditional web application. We also build the portal web role for our sample application in this chapter.

Chapter 10, Web Services and Azure, discusses WCF web services and provides an overview of building a web service. We also build the web service needed for our sample application.

Chapter 11, Worker Roles, speaks about worker roles and many of the functions they can perform. We also build the worker roles for our sample application in this chapter.

Chapter 12, Local Application for Updates, teaches us how to build a Windows Forms application that interacts with our web services.

Chapter 13, Azure AppFabric, provides an overview of the Azure AppFabric, and discusses the capabilities of Access Control and Service Bus. We also configure Access Control for our sample application.

Chapter 14, Azure Monitoring and Diagnostics, discusses the diagnostic monitoring services available in Microsoft Azure, along with how to enable these services in our sample application.

Chapter 15, Deploying to Windows Azure, teaches how to deploy our sample application to Windows Azure and how to change our application's configuration once it is deployed.

What you need for this book

For this book, we need a PC running Windows XP or 7. We also need either Visual Studio 2008 or 2010, or if both are not available, we can go for Visual Web Developer 2010 Express Edition. SQL Server 2008 Express also needs to be installed. We need to install the Windows Azure Tools for Microsoft Visual Studio, and depending on the OS and Visual Studio used, there may be some additional hotfixes. A complete list of requirements can be found at `http://msdn.microsoft.com/en-us/windowsazure/cc974146.aspx`.

Who this book is for

If you are a developer or architect who wants to build enterprise-level applications with Azure, but needs to understand more about Azure's capabilities first, this book is for you. As the examples are in .NET, the book will skew to MS-oriented developers. But a lot of what is discussed will be applicable to anyone wanting to work with Azure. No matter what language you use, you provision the application fabric the same way, and all the underlying concepts will be the same. You will need experience with Visual Studio, and some basic SQL Server knowledge.

Conventions

In this book, you will find a number of styles of text that distinguish between different kinds of information. Here are some examples of these styles, and an explanation of their meaning.

Code words in text are shown as follows: "Because there are no keys to link tables together, the ADO.NET Data Services methods that deal with links are unavailable to use, including AddLink, DetachLink, and SetLink".

A block of code will be set as follows:

```
CREATE TABLE [dbo].[Customers](
    [CustomerID] [int] IDENTITY(1,1) NOT NULL,
    [CustomerName] [varchar](50) NOT NULL,
    [CustomerAddress1] [varchar](50) NOT NULL
```

When we wish to draw your attention to a particular part of a code block, the relevant lines or items will be shown in bold:

```
Imports System.ServiceModel

' NOTE: If you change the class name "IERPService" here, you must also
update the reference to "IERPService" in Web.config.
<ServiceContract()> _
Public Interface IERPService
```

New terms and **important words** are shown in bold. Words that you see on the screen, in menus or dialog boxes for example, appear in our text like this: "The first setting we need to change is, setting the **Script for database engine type** option to the **SQL Azure Database** option, as seen in the following screenshot".

Warnings or important notes appear in a box like this.

 Tips and tricks appear like this.

Reader feedback

Feedback from our readers is always welcome. Let us know what you think about this book—what you liked or may have disliked. Reader feedback is important for us to develop titles that you really get the most out of.

To send us general feedback, simply send an e-mail to feedback@packtpub.com, and mention the book title via the subject of your message.

If there is a book that you need and would like to see us publish, please send us a note in the **SUGGEST A TITLE** form on www.packtpub.com or e-mail suggest@packtpub.com.

If there is a topic that you have expertise in and you are interested in either writing or contributing to a book, see our author guide on www.packtpub.com/authors.

Customer support

Now that you are the proud owner of a Packt book, we have a number of things to help you to get the most from your purchase.

 Downloading the example code for this book
You can download the example code files for all Packt books you have purchased from your account at http://www.PacktPub.com. If you purchased this book elsewhere, you can visit http://www.PacktPub.com/support and register to have the files e-mailed directly to you.

Errata

Although we have taken every care to ensure the accuracy of our content, mistakes do happen. If you find a mistake in one of our books—maybe a mistake in the text or the code—we would be grateful if you would report this to us. By doing so, you can save other readers from frustration and help us improve subsequent versions of this book. If you find any errata, please report them by visiting http://www.packtpub.com/support, selecting your book, clicking on the errata submission form link, and entering the details of your errata. Once your errata are verified, your submission will be accepted and the errata will be uploaded on our website, or added to any list of existing errata, under the Errata section of that title. Any existing errata can be viewed by selecting your title from http://www.packtpub.com/support.

Piracy

Piracy of copyright material on the Internet is an ongoing problem across all media. At Packt, we take the protection of our copyright and licenses very seriously. If you come across any illegal copies of our works, in any form, on the Internet, please provide us with the location address or website name immediately so that we can pursue a remedy.

Please contact us at copyright@packtpub.com with a link to the suspected pirated material.

We appreciate your help in protecting our authors, and our ability to bring you valuable content.

Questions

You can contact us at questions@packtpub.com if you are having a problem with any aspect of the book, and we will do our best to address it.

1

Introduction to Cloud Computing

Cloud computing is a term that has risen to the top of application development discussions in a very short period of time. Amazon, Google, and Microsoft (among many others), all offer cloud-computing services and are not shy about touting its benefits. If you believe the marketing hype, cloud computing ranks somewhere between revolutionary and the second coming of your favorite prophet. But what exactly is cloud computing, and how does it play into the daily lives of enterprise developers? Let's now try and find some answers.

What is an enterprise application?

Before we hop into the cloud, let's talk about who this book is for. Who are "enterprise developers"? In the United States, over half of the economy is small businesses, usually privately owned, with a couple dozen of employees and revenues up to the millions of dollars. The applications that run these businesses have lower requirements because of smaller data volumes and a low number of application users. A single server may host several applications. Many of the business needs for these companies can be met with off-the-shelf software requiring little to no modification.

The minority of the United States economy is made up of huge publicly owned corporations — think Microsoft, Apple, McDonald's, Coca-Cola, Best Buy, and so on. These companies have thousands of employees and revenues in the billions of dollars. Because these companies are publicly owned, they are subject to tight regulatory scrutiny. The applications utilized by these companies must faithfully keep track of an immense amount of data to be utilized by hundreds or thousands of users, and must comply with all matters of regulations. The infrastructure for a single application may involve dozens of servers. A team of consultants is often retained to install and maintain the critical systems of a business, and there is often an ecosystem of internal applications built around the enterprise systems that are just as critical. These are the applications we consider to be "enterprise applications", and the people who develop and extend them are "enterprise developers". The high availability of cloud platforms makes them attractive for hosting these critical applications, and there are many options available to the enterprise developer. This books focuses on Microsoft's cloud development platform named Azure. Throughout this book, we'll develop a simple example application as an introduction to the different facets of Microsoft's Windows Azure platform, and we'll also discuss concepts useful to the enterprise developer, including security and costs, during the course of our application's development.

What is cloud computing?

At its most basic, cloud computing is moving applications accessible from our internal network onto an internet (cloud)-accessible space. We're essentially renting virtual machines in someone else's data center, with the capabilities for immediate scale-out, failover, and data synchronization. In the past, having an Internet-accessible application meant we were building a website with a hosted database. Cloud computing changes that paradigm—our application could be a website, or it could be a client installed on a local PC accessing a common data store from anywhere in the world. The data store could be internal to our network or itself hosted in the cloud. The following diagram outlines three ways in which cloud computing can be utilized for an application. In option 1, both data and application have been hosted in the cloud, the second option is to host our application in the cloud and our data locally, and the third option is to host our data in the cloud and our application locally.

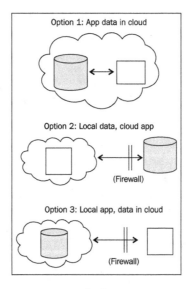

The expense (or cost) model is also very different. In our local network, we have to buy the hardware and software licenses, install and configure the servers, and finally we have to maintain them. All this counts in addition to building and maintaining the application! In cloud computing, the host usually handles all the installation, configuration, and maintenance of the servers, allowing us to focus mostly on the application. The direct costs of running our application in the cloud are only for each machine-hour of use and storage utilization.

The individual pieces of cloud computing have all been around for some time. Shared mainframes and supercomputers have for a long time billed the end users based on that user's resource consumption. Space for websites can be rented on a monthly basis. Providers offer specialized application hosting and, relatively recently, leased virtual machines have also become available. If there is anything revolutionary about cloud computing, then it is its ability to combine all the best features of these different components into a single affordable service offering.

Some benefits of cloud computing

Cloud computing sounds great so far, right? So, what are some of the tangible benefits of cloud computing? Does cloud computing merit all the attention? Let's have a look at some of the advantages:

- **Low up-front cost**:

  At the top of the benefits list is probably the low up-front cost. With cloud computing, someone else is buying and installing the servers, switches, and firewalls, among other things. In addition to the hardware, software licenses and assurance plans are also expensive on the enterprise level, even with a purchasing agreement. In most cloud services, including Microsoft's Azure platform, we do not need to purchase separate licenses for operating systems or databases. In Azure, the costs include licenses for Windows Azure OS and SQL Azure. As a corollary, someone else is responsible for the maintenance and upkeep of the servers — no more tape backups that must be rotated and sent to off-site storage, no extensive strategies and lost weekends bringing servers up to the current release level, and no more counting the minutes until the early morning delivery of a hot swap fan to replace the one that burned out the previous afternoon.

- **Easier disaster recovery and storage management**:

  With synchronized storage across multiple data centers, located in different regions in the same country or even in different countries, disaster recovery planning becomes significantly easier.

If capacity needs to be increased, it can be done quite easily by logging into a control panel and turning on an additional VM. It would be a rare instance indeed when our provider doesn't sell us additional capacity. When the need for capacity passes, we can simply turn off the VMs we no longer need and pay only for the uptime and storage utilization.

- **Simplified migration**:

  Migration from a test to a production environment is greatly simplified. In Windows Azure, we can test an updated version of our application in a local sandbox environment. When we're ready to go live, we deploy our application to a staged environment in the cloud and, with a few mouse clicks in the control panel, we turn off the live virtual machine and activate the staging environment as the live machine—we barely miss a beat! The migration can be performed well in advance of the cut-over, so daytime migrations and midnight cut-overs can become routine. Should something go wrong, the environments can be easily reversed and the issues analyzed the following day.

- **Familiar environment**:

  Finally, the environment we're working on is very familiar. In Azure's case, the environment can include the capabilities of IIS and .NET (or Java or PHP and Apache), with Windows and SQL Server or MySQL. One of the great features of Windows is that it can be configured in so many ways, and to an extent, Azure can also be configured in many ways, supporting a rich and familiar application environment.

Some downsides of cloud computing

Cloud computing sounds wonderful so far, but nothing is perfect. There are aspects of cloud computing that will involve compromising, and in some cases, may make cloud computing infeasible for a company; let's have a look at a few of those:

- **Less control on application environment**:

  One of the biggest concerns is that we are no longer in control of our application environment. Giving up control over the maintenance of the firewalls, servers, and operating system can be troubling, especially for sensitive institutions such as health or banking. We are now storing data and our application in a publicly accessible space. There is the possibility of a data breach through some means other than our application. To address these two concerns, services and plans calling themselves "private clouds" are beginning to enter the marketplace. These private clouds will partition our space in a secure way from prying eyes but still allow us the level of access, uptime, and backup we desire from the cloud.

With someone else in control of the patch level of the operating system, testing against new updates becomes an ongoing process. None of us have ever had application issues resulting from a security update, right? The good news is, we can have snapshots of production environments, which can be used to test patches. This makes it significantly easier to have a test system that replicates production.

- **Higher costs**:

  For many web-based applications, the costs for a cloud application are probably higher than standard shared hosting. Based on the pricing announced at PDC 2009, a simple website application with a single instance would cost around $100/month to host, compared to around $5-$20/month for standard shared hosting.

- **Difficulty with hosting**:

  Finally, in most cases, hosting an application in the cloud is not as simple as just deploying to a remote server. For existing applications, there may be some significant changes, such as replacing local connection strings with a service-oriented architecture, or utilizing high-performance storage such as tables and blobs rather than file system storage. Hopefully, the rest of this book will help diminish any differences between a local and a cloud application.

Cloud computing infrastructure

Cloud computing requires more than just a server room, and the different providers employ different technologies. In all cases, cloud computing relies on data centers in multiple geographic locations, with multiple redundancies of everything. It's quite a challenge to locate an area that is geologically stable and relatively free from severe weather events or other natural disasters, making redundancies of locations, in addition to redundancies of utilities, a necessity.

Cloud data centers have moved away from the "racks-in-a-room" or "raised floor" design of traditional data centers. One of the more common designs for cloud data centers is to modify a shipping container to hold racks of servers, and then linking multiple containers together into a large center. The container-based design is used more for stability, space efficiency, and physical isolation of machines. A forty-foot tall rack of servers would be highly unstable and extremely difficult to manage. But a stack of four containers is very stable, and each container is as easy to manage as a small server room. It's also more efficient to cool a number of small rooms as compared to a giant warehouse.

For Azure, Microsoft has taken the container concept a little farther. Microsoft's Azure containers (called Generation 4 Modular Data Centers or G4MDC) are not based on a shipping container, although the end design resembles one. Technically, Microsoft's containers are classified as air handling units and the servers as heaters. Cooling is achieved by pulling outside air through filters, into the container, and around the servers at high velocity. In fact, some of Microsoft's new data centers won't even have roofs! Each G4MDC unit is completely self-contained with airflow regulation, and its own connections for power and bandwidth. Each 40-foot unit can accommodate up to 2,000 servers, and some of Microsoft's facilities will house 400,000 to 500,000 servers.

Cloudy skies ahead

Usually, cloudy skies are a bad thing—many a day at the beach has been ruined by an abundance of clouds. But in the case of cloud computing, the more clouds, the better! The number of providers of cloud computing services is increasing, but for the enterprise developer, the three major options at the time of writing are from Google, Amazon, and Microsoft.

Google's cloud offering is named the Google AppEngine, and currently supports Python and Java languages. Data are stored in the Google AppEngine data store, a proprietary database utilizing **Google Query Language** (**GQL**). For the interested developer, Google offers a free plan with multiple applications.

Amazon has several cloud offerings, all under the Amazon Web Services umbrella, including Simple DB, Elastic Compute Cloud (EC2), Simple Storage Service (S3), and Amazon Virtual Private Cloud (VPC). Simple DB and S3 are data-storage options that are used for everything from compressed backup locations to simple content delivery networks. EC2 is a service that allows us to create a virtual machine to our specifications, and upload it to our cloud-hosting account. We are still completely responsible for the care and feeding of our VM, but Amazon provides the hosting infrastructure. The Amazon VPC is our own private IP block carved out of Amazon's Web Services. The Amazon VPC can be made part of our local network by means of VPN from our firewall to our isolated cloud storage, gaining much of the benefits of cloud storage with the convenience of a local network resource.

Last but not least (and the star of this book) is Microsoft's Azure. **Azure** actually comprises three services, each of which can be used independently or combined into a completely cloud-based application. When most people speak of Azure, they're speaking of Windows Azure, which is the operating system, application hosting as well as simple storage services. The second piece of Azure is one that has generated a great deal of excitement—SQL Azure. SQL Azure is an almost feature complete version of SQL Server 2008. The final piece of the Windows Azure platform is the

AppFabric, which provides connection and authentication services along with the **Service Bus**—an enterprise service bus implementation capable of bridging two different enterprises.

Is cloud computing "enterprisey" enough?

There have been many products and services making great promises to the enterprise developer, and a lot of the chatter about cloud computing at times makes it seem like this is yet another buzzword that will pass. Looking at the companies that have made the move to the various cloud platforms makes us think otherwise. Even before its official release, companies such as Domino's, Kelly Blue Book, and Coca-Cola Enterprises had already adapted applications for Azure, and many more case studies were posted from PDC 2009. To underscore the flexibility of the Azure platform, Domino's application is written in Java and served by Tomcat.

No cloud computing platform can be all things to all people. Each platform differs in its capabilities and service offerings, and price can be a factor as well. Enterprise applications typically include a database back end, and Google's lack of a relational database and limited language support (Python and some flavors of Java) make it a tough sell for enterprises that require a full database and use .NET technologies. With Amazon's services, we need to build our own virtual machine (or start with a pre-built one), but we are still responsible for licensing costs, removing the price advantage. Microsoft's Azure platform is designed to be a very happy medium—a wide range of languages can be used, there are no licensing costs, and Azure has some advanced features such as Access Control and Service Bus not found in other cloud offerings. One thing is for sure—with three big players in the cloud computing game, the services will become more feature rich, less expensive, and in the end, the consumers will benefit greatly.

The presence of so many large applications in the cloud is not proof positive enough to conclude that cloud computing is the way of the future, but such rapid adoption speaks well of the advantages of cloud-based applications, especially the time to develop them. The promise of cloud computing platforms is that they are stable, scalable, easy to develop, and are cost effective. Time will tell which providers perform the best, but even at this early stage there are plenty of case studies to observe.

Summary

This chapter served as an overview of cloud computing, from a definition to covering a few advantages and disadvantages. We delved a little into the physical infrastructure of a cloud data center and finished up with a brief overview of the three main enterprise providers (Google, Amazon, and Microsoft). The cloud computing offerings have emerged and grown in a very short period of time, sparking not only a great deal of conversation, but also a fair amount of adoption.

2
The Nickel Tour of Azure

So, we're enterprise developers, architecting an application to enhance some core business processes. The decision makers need more information about Azure before they're sold on a cloud-based application. They want to know what can Azure do, will we be able to include all the features we need, and will it cost more to develop for Azure?

Microsoft's marketing group tends to work with a thin thesaurus, so if you're a fan of confusing product names, Microsoft does not disappoint with their Azure offering. We'll clear up the mystery of three Azures and four fabrics.

This chapter is by no means an exhaustive answer to the questions that will be raised and, as the technology is changing so rapidly, it's important to augment this chapter with some additional research before committing to any features of the application.

Explaining Azure to the managers

We aren't all graced by management with a strong technical background, and yet they need a deeper dive into the shallow end to achieve a win-win situation and obtain senior management buy-in to leverage this new platform. Sometimes, it's like you actually do work in the same office as Dilbert.

As we mentioned before, Microsoft Azure actually refers to a menu of services offered by Microsoft; each of these services is contained in the Azure Fabric. The Azure Fabric is essentially every piece of hardware and the software that monitors and controls the hardware. Every server, every firewall, every load balancer, failover services in the event of a failure, the Azure portal where we provision and deploy our application, create and check the health of our current services — they're all part of the Azure Fabric. Fabric in this case has a very large definition — as far as the Azure universe is concerned, the Azure Fabric is the continuum of space and time.

The three items on the Azure menu are Windows Azure, SQL Azure, and the AppFabric. The following diagram shows how these items interrelate with one another, as well as with applications and databases separate from Microsoft Azure. For the remainder of this book, when we refer to Azure, we will be talking about the menu of services. When we discuss a specific item, we'll refer to it using its specific name such as Windows Azure or SQL Azure.

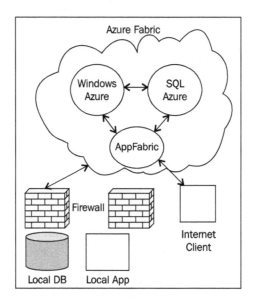

One of the most interesting features of Azure is the support for a number of languages and web servers. Many people mistakenly think that because Azure is a Microsoft offering, its usage is limited to .NET and IIS. Nothing could be further from the truth! In addition to .NET 4.0 (including .NET 2.0, 3.0, and 3.5), Azure also supports PHP, C++, and Java, as well as Ruby and Ruby on Rails. There is also choice in the databases and development environments. Web servers include IIS, Apache, and Tomcat; databases include SQL Server (via SQL Azure) and MySQL; and development tools include all versions of Visual Studio 2008/2010, Visual Studio Web Developer 2008/2010 Express, and Eclipse—that's a lot of choice! SDKs, toolkits, and plugins are provided for the more common options and others are being developed. Azure supports .NET 4, ASP.NET MVC and Silverlight, and new features are being added in an ongoing basis.

Microsoft has an expanding number of data centers around the world. For compliance purposes, you can select the data center in which your application will reside, or locate your application close by to take advantage of regional prices. Your application is replicated multiple times across the data center of your choosing; so, if there is a hardware failure on the primary instance, the load balancer will direct the traffic to an instance that is alive and healthy!

Windows Azure

The service offering that has commonly been referred to as Azure is actually Windows Azure. For the rest of this book, when we refer to Azure, we'll call it Windows Azure.

Windows Azure is just what it sounds like—it is the operating system part of the cloud, with a few other features. The most inflexible part of the Azure universe is the fact that Windows Azure is not designed to provide customized virtual machines; (custom VHDs are a newly announced offering at PDC10, but are a different service than Windows Azure) we are limited to a 64-bit version of Windows Server 2008. We can create VMs of different sizes (the sizes relate to costs), and the OS is highly configurable, but it must remain Windows.

Windows Azure encompasses two areas of functionality—the compute service and the storage service. The next diagram shows how these services fit into the Azure universe. Additionally, there is an Azure Fabric Agent that connects the VM to the rest of the cloud. The Fabric Controller is a modified version of the Windows Server 2008 Hyper-V hypervisor, which sits in between our VM and the hardware, allowing resources to be used by the VM. There is a service that runs on all VMs, communicating the status of the VM back to the Fabric Controller, allowing the Fabric Controller to monitor for faults. Should a VM communicate a fault, the Fabric Controller can initiate a sequence of events to try and get the VM back to the proper status. This could be anything from a VM reboot to a new VM provisioning.

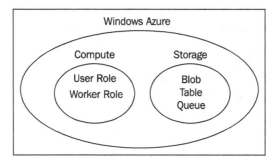

Compute service

The compute service can be thought of as the actual application code. Applications are further broken down into **web** roles and **worker** roles. Web roles are website applications, whereas worker roles are analogous to services on a local PC or server. Application users interact with web roles, while worker roles perform functions behind the scenes. Worker roles can interact with web roles, but application users cannot directly interact with a worker role (except in one special case, which we'll see later).

Worker roles are a separate entity from the web roles. They are a completely separate VM and act independently of each other. It is possible for a worker role to exist without a web role, just as a web role may exist without a worker role.

Storage service

For local storage of files (both small files consisting of a few kilobytes to large files up to terabytes) and simple data, we have to rely on the storage services. There are three components to the storage service: **blob**, **table**, and **queue**. Each has its own purpose, and we may use any combination of these components or none at all. Storage services can be used to build a highly scalable system as the amount of data and file storage is virtually endless (though every increase in storage space used comes with an increase of monthly cost). Given the way Windows Azure works, we'll more than likely use at least one of these services in any given application, and our sample application will use all three.

On Windows Azure, the local file system is not persistent, so our application needs to store and retrieve its resources from a floating storage location. Data placed in the storage service is persisted if a VM is shut down or if new VMs are brought online. For safety, all storage service data is replicated three times.

If this sounds unnecessary or confusing, think of the storage service options like a roaming profile. Unlike some cloud computing options, an Azure VM is not dedicated to us or our application. They are more like the PCs in the college computer lab. One day you may find space on one PC, and another day you have to use a different PC. If we saved information on the file system on one PC, we wouldn't have access to it on days where we sat at a different PC, and we probably wouldn't want others to access our files when they use the same machine where we stored them. If we turn our Azure application off and then on again, or switch between a staging and production VM, we're actually changing VMs. We need our information to be available immediately, and preferably without a great deal of work to distribute it—hence, the floating storage service.

Blob Storage

Blob is an abbreviation for **binary large object**. Blob Storage is designed to contain large amounts of binary data such as images, music files, or complete documents and spreadsheets. Blobs are stored in containers, and each container can be up to 50 GB and contain a number of blobs. Up to 8 KB of metadata can be stored with each container in name/value pairs (note that metadata is at the container level, not the individual blob).

If an Azure-based web application displays a logo, that logo will be called from a Blob Storage endpoint, rather than a local file. We could also build a document management system or content management system using Blob Storage. To access a blob, we use a standard REST interface or a .NET client library.

Table Storage

This is the part where people get the most confused with all the Azure options. Windows Azure Table Storage is *not* the same as SQL Azure. Table Storage is not relational, does not have a defined schema, and does not use a query language for data access. In contrast, SQL Azure is an almost feature complete version of SQL Server 2008.

Table Storage operates more like a hash table or an indexed array. We do connect to table storage using ADO.NET Data Services, and we can also retrieve data through either Linq or REST. Table Storage can be used to store all manner of data, with a capacity of terabytes. Table properties (columns or values) can be strongly typed to a number of data types, and data is partitioned to improve scalability. Despite the large capacity of a table, the total combined size of the properties in a record can be a maximum of 1 MB.

Tables are created and managed programmatically from code we build, and although they seem limited, tables are actually a powerful storage method. A single table in Table Storage can actually contain more data than a single SQL Azure database, and contents can be loaded into generic or strongly types objects for ease of programming.

Queue Storage

Queue Storage is unlike the previous two storage services. In Windows Azure, a queue is a holding area for requests waiting to be processed by a worker role. Web roles interact with worker roles by adding requests to the queue. Unlike tables and blobs, which persist data for repetitive use, the Queue Storage is a container for transient data. One example of a common use could be the usage of Queue Storage to deposit messages based on events that occurred. Here, a worker role can pick these messages on a timed interval and perform event-based workflows, coded into the worker role, based on the message contents.

Each Windows Azure account can have multiple queues, and each queue can contain up to 8 KB of metadata in addition to the requests. Queue Storage is accessed via a REST interface, or .NET client library and can be accessed by any client with the correct storage credentials for the account.

Azure Fabric Agent and Controller

The Azure Fabric Agent is one of four things that have "fabric" in their name in the Microsoft Azure menu. The Windows Azure Fabric is part of the overall Azure Fabric, and is an interface between the Azure Fabric Controller and the individual VM and the VM's contents.

SQL Azure

Originally known as *SQL Data Services*, SQL Azure for many people is the most exciting item on the Microsoft Azure menu.

SQL Azure is an almost feature complete implementation of SQL Server 2008 Geographic data types are now supported. Unlike Table Storage, SQL Azure is completely relational, with a defined schema, supports T-SQL, and we can connect via ADO.NET or ODBC.

We can manage our SQL Azure databases through the SQL Azure Portal, directly via sqlcmd, or through SQL Server Management Studio 2008 R2. At the time of writing, SQL Server 2008 R2 is the most recent release of SQL Server, and is the only **SQL Server Management Studio** (**SSMS**) version that can completely connect to SQL Azure. Microsoft provides a SQL Azure Database Manager (formerly known as Project Houston), an online tool that is used to manage SQL Azure databases. There are also a couple of third-party tools, such as SQL Azure Manager and the Omega Web Client, for managing SQL Azure. Undoubtedly, more tools will arise as more people begin to work with SQL Azure. The SQL Azure Manager (though in Alpha testing at the time of writing) can be found at `http://hanssens.org/post/SQL-Azure-Manager.aspx`. The Omega Web Client (along with other great third-party tools for Azure) can be found at `http://www.cerebrata.com`.

Just as with SQL Server, we can have multiple databases per SQL Azure instance. Database sizes are limited, so if it's possible our application may exceed the maximum size, it's a good idea to either build in an archiving strategy and tools, or plan for a multiple SQL Azure account and multiple database solution at the beginning. Behind the scenes, and just like the storage options in Windows Azure, SQL Azure data is replicated three times to ensure availability and backup.

SQL Azure Data Sync is scheduled for final release soon. Formerly known as Project Huron, SQL Azure Data Sync enables synchronization of data between SQL Azure instances, or SQL Azure and on premises SQL Server databases.

Windows Azure platform: AppFabric

AppFabric is another part of Azure with "fabric" in its name. AppFabric was originally known as BizTalk Services, and then later as .NET Services. Unlike the Azure Fabric or the Azure Fabric Agent, AppFabric is not a low-level controller/ manager of the virtual machines. Instead, AppFabric provides the Service Bus, Access Control services, and connection components.

The Service Bus is the functionality that serves as a bridge between on-premises applications and Windows Azure. The Service Bus also facilitates bidirectional communication between two non-Azure applications.

Bridging local and Azure applications is useful in certain cases such as if there is information in our local **warehouse management system (WMS)** we want to make visible to our clients via an Azure-based portal we develop. If our WMS has an API we'd like to manifest directly to our partners, we can also use the Service Bus to abstract the WMS API. In this case, we'd register our WMS's endpoint with the Service Bus, which would then create a public set of its own endpoints. We'd provide the Azure endpoint URIs to our partners to be consumed by their applications. When a call is made against the public endpoints, Azure queues that client request and passes it to our WMS. Our WMS responds to Azure's request, and Azure sends the data on to our partner. The Azure Service Bus handles the discovery and registration of the endpoints, and handles the NAT as well. In terms of securing our WMS, no one needs to know our private IP address, and we limit our firewall to a smaller list of IPs to allow through.

In the Service Bus examples, we'd obviously need a way to limit access to the application or endpoints. This is one of many places where the Access Control functionality of AppFabric is important. Access Control issues security tokens that can be consumed by Azure and non-Azure applications via REST (SOAP has been announced but was not in place at the time of writing). Access Control is a claims-based identity service, similar to OpenID or Microsoft's LiveID.

AppFabric also incorporates projects codenamed *Dublin* and *Velocity*. Both Dublin and Velocity are standalone projects that can be used with both Azure and more traditional applications. At the time of writing, these projects were announced but not released, so more detailed information should be gathered directly from Microsoft. Project Dublin is an effort to enhance the management of .NET 4 WCF and WF services as well as IIS management and monitoring. Dublin utilizes PowerShell commandlets and IIS integration.

 It is useful to note that AppFabric can be used separately from the other parts of Azure, and its components can be used individually from one another.

Codename Dallas

Project Dallas is Microsoft's entry into the new data-as-a-service (DaaS) market. The goal of Dallas is to provide a single authoritative source and a single billing method for public data. Think of Dallas as a "data marketplace", where we can buy subscriptions to data useful for our applications, and where data providers can sell their data.

The data in Dallas are accessible via a REST API, and can be consumed by applications on any platform. Support will be for SQL Server and SQL Azure to directly consume Dallas data, but this has not been delivered at the time of writing.

More information on Codename Dallas can be found at http://www.microsoft.com/windowsazure/dallas/.

Development Fabric

The Development Fabric is yet another part of Azure with "fabric" in its name. The Development Fabric is a specialized Windows Azure environment used for local development. It is akin to the Azure Fabric, but is hosted on a single local machine. We install the Development Fabric with the Windows Azure SDK and other tools. We'll use the Development Fabric as we create our sample application through the rest of this book.

Considerations for the ASP.NET developer

It's easy to think developing a web role is just the same as developing a traditional website, but that's not the case. The web role is not just a website, but a complete ASP.NET web application. If we have multiple instances of our web role application running, the Azure load balancer doesn't guarantee a user's connections will all be made on the same VM. One consequence of this is that our application should either be stateless, or use the database (or table/blob) or cookies to maintain session state. In-process session state isn't an option.

Imagine a local web farm with a load balancer that does not maintain session state. The ideal solution in this case would be to use some type of session storage to maintain state across servers. This is also the case with Windows Azure web role instances. We cannot maintain state in-process if we bounce between machines; however, the state can be shared using our table/blob storage or our SQL Azure service. While we can attach our debugger to our local instance of the Development Fabric, we cannot debug applications remotely that have been deployed in Windows

Azure. We will need to maintain our logging and use it to debug issues, if present in the cloud. Because we are not guaranteed to browse our web application on the same server after every call, there is no persistence with local storage. Microsoft answers this issue quickly with table and blob storage. All data and files that need to be accessible need to be saved in a storage service or a SQL Azure database (the highly scalable option is using storage services).

How are Azure costs calculated?

Microsoft Azure has two methods for calculating the monthly service charges—consumption pricing or commitment (subscription) pricing. Because Windows Azure, SQL Azure, and AppFabric are three independent services, each is priced separately and with its own rates. The charges may seem like nickel-and-diming as they are broken out by the different features of each service, but having the charges broken out allows us to utilize and pay for only what we use.

In addition to production-scale pricing plans, Microsoft also offers limited-use plans suitable for development and conference room pilot efforts. For the most current rates and offers, visit http://www.microsoft.com/windowsazure/pricing/. We're not going to list the base rates here, as they are likely to change over time. Instead, we'll look at how the charges are applied to each service in the next section.

Cloud services such as Amazon EC2 bill in a manner close to what Microsoft does, yet offer a little more flexibility with types of VMs (they offer both UNIX/Linux pricing and Windows pricing, which varies based on the type of hosting needed). They also offer commitment plans, but theirs is called "Reserve Instances". This is where a flat fee is paid up front, based on a time commitment, but a reduced usage fee is charged on a monthly basis.

Calculating Windows Azure pricing

Windows Azure charges are calculated based on utilization of four resources—compute time, storage, storage transactions, and data transfers.

Compute time is billed as service hours or the amount of time an application is deployed. When calculating compute time charges, keep in mind each instance of an application runs in its own VM. If we have two instances of an application running simultaneously for an hour, that is calculated as two service hours of compute time.

Storage is billed as the daily average gigabytes consumed in the storage service (tables and blobs). To minimize costs, we want to minimize the size of resources we store for a long duration. If we have a 30 GB blob in storage for a month, our average daily consumption would be 30 GB. If we were to upload a 30 GB blob for a single day, our average consumption would be 1 GB.

Storage transactions are the CRUD operations we perform against tables and blobs. Every `create`, `read`, `update`, and `delete` operation we perform against our data is a transaction.

Data transfers are billed as the total number of gigabytes uploaded or downloaded via the Internet during a month. Any communication within sub-region (same data center) is not charged. This is helpful for HTTP calls between different services, and also emphasizes the correct usage of Affinity Groups (discussed in *Chapter 15, Deploying to Windows Azure*) to keep dependent services together.

The other transactions are application requests, and pass through the Queue Storage. At the time of writing, there was no specific charge for application requests.

Calculating SQL Azure pricing

SQL Azure is sold in two editions—Web and Business—plus data transfers. SQL Azure databases are billed monthly but calculated per diem, and we are only charged for the days we have the database.

Both editions are self managed and support Visual Studio, SQL Server Management Studio, and SQL Server Integration Services. The Web Edition has a capacity of up to 5 GB, while the Business Edition has a capacity of up to 50 GB and supports advanced features such as auto-partition and upcoming plans for **common language runtime (CLR)** integration.

As with Windows Azure, data transfers are calculated as the total number of gigabytes uploaded or downloaded via the Internet during a billing month.

Calculating AppFabric pricing

AppFabric charges are billed by Access Control transactions, Service Bus connections, and data transfer.

Each claim of identity made to the Access Control service is a transaction. Charges are calculated based on the actual number of transactions during a billing month.

Service Bus connections are sold as individual pay-as-you-go connections, or can be purchased in flat-rate packs. Individual connections are charged based on the maximum number of connections utilized during a day. Connection packs are calculated daily, based on the pro-rata number of connections. If we buy a 30-pack of connections at the beginning of a month and then buy another 30-pack one week in, we are charged for 7 connection days for the first week, and then 14 connection days thereafter.

As with Windows Azure, data transfers are calculated as the total number of gigabytes uploaded or downloaded via the Internet during a billing month.

Summary

In this chapter, we had a quick look at the features of Microsoft Azure and how to calculate the costs of the Microsoft Azure platform. From Windows Azure, to SQL Azure, to Dallas, Microsoft has a complete and useful cloud offering. We'll spend the rest of this book examining most of these features of Windows Azure, SQL Azure, and AppFabric in greater depth, and building a sample application using these features.

3
Setting Up for Development

Now that we've learned the high-level concepts and benefits of cloud computing and Windows Azure in the previous two chapters, the next question in our mind should be "How do I create my applications for the Windows Azure cloud?" To fabricate anything, we must have the right tools at hand. In this chapter, we'll discuss and install the tools necessary for local development of Windows Azure.

Downloading the tools

In order to build an Azure application, we need a framework to access the underlying classes, a development environment, and possibly a few hotfixes as well. The downloads necessary vary by OS (32 or 64 bit, XP or 7), language choice (.NET or PHP), and development environment (Visual Studio or Eclipse). The most current list of tools needed for Azure development is available at `http://msdn.microsoft.com/en-us/windowsazure/cc974146.aspx`.

Configuring the local machine for development

First, let's talk about operating systems; more specifically, the operating systems supported by the Windows Azure Development Fabric. Windows Azure is a relatively new platform, released to the world in February 2010 as a production environment. It was developed after the release of Windows Vista, and Windows Vista SP1 is the earliest supported operating system for local development. Windows Vista SP1, Windows 7, and Windows Server 2008 are also supported for local development. The Windows Azure Tools for Microsoft Visual Studio will install a local Development Fabric and development storage, which allows us to develop, test, and debug locally without pushing our application into the cloud. We can think of the local development fabric and storage as an Azure emulator. The Development

Fabric (and other local tools) requires one of the Windows operating systems mentioned above. When it's time to deploy our application, we'll use these same tools to package our application for deployment.

Once we determine that we have a supported OS, the next thing we need to do is install the .NET Framework, enable Internet Information Services (IIS) 7.0 (or later) features, and enable Windows Communication Foundation (WCF) HTTP activation. To check the latest version of the .NET Framework, we can use a registry editor tool, or the `regedit` command to check the registry settings, at **HKEY_LOCAL_ MACHINE | SOFTWARE | Microsoft | NET Framework Setup | NDP**. You will see each version installed. If v4 or higher is installed, there is nothing else to check. If **v3.5** is the highest version listed, select that registry section to view the registry values. We need to make sure we have version 3.5.30729.01 or higher, which is the version for the .NET 3.5 SP1 Framework. If the .NET 3.5 SP1Framework or later is not installed, you will need to download from `http://www.microsoft.com/net/` and install the framework. The registry will appear similar to the following screenshot:

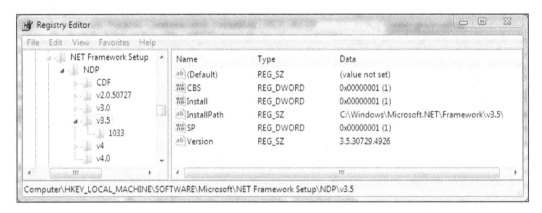

An alternative to using a registry tool is to open Internet Explorer and enter `javascript:alert(navigator.userAgent)` into the address bar (this command doesn't work in other browsers). This will open a modal dialog with the entire user-agent values, including the .NET Framework version. The modal dialog looks similar to the next screenshot. Note that earlier versions of the .NET framework report as **.NET CLR**, but version 4 reports as simply **.NET**.

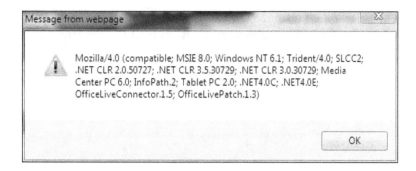

Next, we need to enable IIS features. To do this, we will need to go to the **Control Panel | Programs | Turn Windows features on or off**. In the **Windows Features** box shown in the next screenshot, expand **Internet Information Systems | World Wide Web Services | Application Development Features** and make sure the boxes beside **ASP.NET** and **CGI** are checked. The CGI option installs both CGI and FastCGI, and is necessary to host PHP applications on IIS. Additionally, FastCGI aids performance when multiple versions of the same framework are installed on IIS. CGI is an optional IIS feature, but it is recommended to enable it.

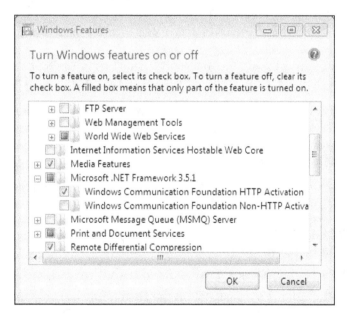

To enable WCF HTTP Activation, expand **Microsoft .NET Framework 3.5.1** and make sure **Windows Communication Foundation HTTP Activation** is checked, as seen in the screenshot:

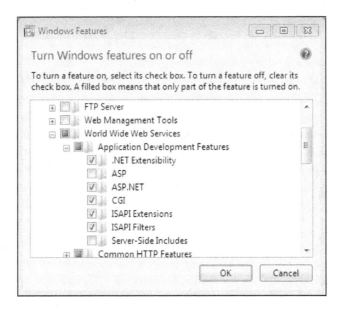

Our development platform will be Microsoft Visual Studio 2008 SP1, though the free Microsoft Visual Web Developer 2008 SP1 is supported, as is Visual Studio 2010.

In addition to Visual Studio 2008, we need to have Microsoft SQL Server 2005/2008 Express or higher installed. This is also a free application from Microsoft. Typically, this is installed with Visual Studio unless a custom install is done and this option was not selected for installation.

Once we have our development and database environments installed, there are a few Microsoft hotfixes that may need to be applied:

- **KB967631**: Update for Visual Studio 2008 SP1 Debugger (not needed for Visual Studio 2010)

- **KB963676**: Improve Visual Studio Stability (not needed on Windows 7)

- **KB967131**: Support for FastCGI on the Development Fabric (not needed for Windows 7 or Windows Server 2008 SP2 Operating Systems)

Again, the required hotfixes depend on the OS and IDE version, and the most up-to-date list can be found at `http://msdn.microsoft.com/en-us/windowsazure/cc974146.aspx`.

Installing Windows Azure tools and SDK

We've finally reached the point where we're about to start installing Windows Azure-specific features and tools. The installation of each of these is very straightforward.

The first thing to install is the Windows Azure Platform Training Kit. This training kit includes presentations, demos, and hands-on labs from Microsoft, targeted at Windows Azure Platform, SQL Azure, and .NET Services. The training kit can be downloaded directly from Microsoft. Once you download the file from Microsoft and execute the application, you will see the following **EULA (End User License Agreement)**. Read over the EULA and click **Accept** to begin installation. Choose your install location and click **Install.**

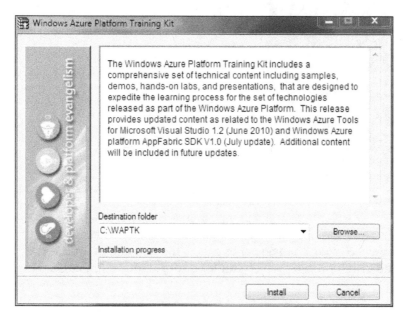

That's it for installing the Windows Azure Platform Training Kit. What's next? We need to install the Windows Azure Tools and SDK, which will add the necessary pieces of the development platform to your local machine. This is also a simple download from Microsoft and has a very simplified installation. Once downloaded, execute the application, click **Next** in the installation wizard, read the EULA, check the box next to **I have read and accept the license terms**, and click **Next** to begin the installation.

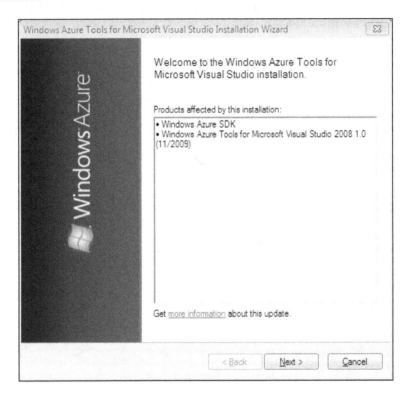

On the next screen, we confirm what we are installing and accept the EULA. This is your last chance to make changes, or to cancel the installation quickly. Clicking **Next** will begin the install process, which can take approximately 10 to 15 minutes.

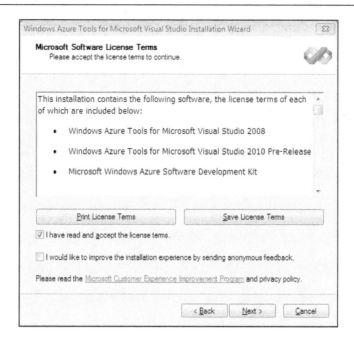

Once this installation is complete, we can now open Visual Studio and we should see new project types. To check, open Visual Studio (or Visual Web Developer), click **File | New Project...** and we should see **Cloud Service** as a project type and a **Windows Azure Cloud Service** template, as we see in the next screenshot:

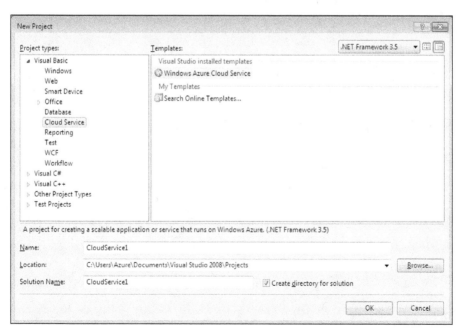

We have now finished preparing our development environment on our local machines! Now that we're done with this, it's time to dig into the fun work!

Summary

In this chapter, we prepared our local systems for development with the necessary tools, SDK, and a training kit prepared by Microsoft to expedite the learning experience, to give us the tools we need, and get us ready to start developing our enterprise application.

4
Designing our Sample Application

Like any project in real life, we start with the business requirements. At Jupiter Motors, we build custom **recreational vehicles** (**RVs**). We've recently opened a new state-of-the-art assembly plant, and implemented a new **Enterprise Resource Planning** (**ERP**) solution. Jupiter Motors now wants to build a customer portal to improve our relationship with our customers, and our team is tasked with building this portal. In this chapter, we'll outline the business processes and portal features relevant to our project, as well as the reasons we've chosen Azure. We'll also sign up for our Azure account.

Project design

All RV sales are handled by independent dealers, who work with our customers and place the customers' orders directly into our ERP system using remote terminals. All orders are reviewed by a production manager, and are approved for production or sent back to the dealer for revision. Once an order has been approved, it should become visible on the portal to the customer.

Assembly begins, and as the process may take several weeks, we want to upload photos of the RV while it's being assembled so that impatient customers can watch the progress. Assembly teams at each stage of the process are responsible for uploading photos as they finish their work.

When the assembly is complete, a driver will deliver the RV to the customer. The customer inspects the RV, and accepts the delivery by signing a tablet PC carried by the driver.

After looking at this summary, we know our customer portal will need the following components:

- A mechanism to transfer data from our ERP system to the portal.
- A database on the portal to hold the transferred data.
- A way to upload and store photographs of the RV.
- User interface for the customers to view their RV.
- Ability to print copies of their order.
- Some way to make sure only customers can log in to the portal.
- A way to make sure the customers can see only their vehicle and order details.
- Serve as an intermediary between customer acceptances and the ERP system. Delivery drivers will update the order in our portal when a customer accepts delivery, and a process in the ERP system will retrieve acceptances and update the ERP system.
- A debug mode, where we can trace events in case there are issues.

An overview of the information flow is shown in the next diagram:

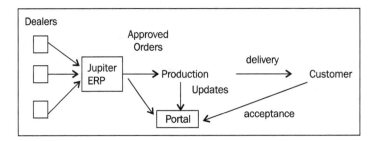

Why are we choosing Azure for our portal? Presumably, we want to use Azure for reasons other than it being the "shiny new thing". Some of the reasons we've decided to use Azure are:

- We're already familiar with Visual Studio, SQL Server, and .NET, so Azure will be familiar to us. Even if we were Java or PHP developers, the Eclipse toolkits and SDKs mean that our skills would still transfer to Azure.
- In this project, storage and retrieval of photos are a principal component. When compared to storing photos in a SQL Server database or on a file system, Blob hosting is easy to use and cost effective.
- Photos require a great deal of bandwidth, and Azure has a **content delivery network (CDN)** we could utilize if necessary.

- Other companies (for example, Outback—a case study can be found at `http://www.microsoft.com/caseStudies/Case_Study_Detail.aspx?cas estudyid=4000005861`) have had great success with Azure social sites. They were able to scale their sites as traffic increased, and could quickly scale to handle traffic spikes.

- There is talk of adding videos, message boards, and other social features to the site, and the Azure platform helps us add these features—in short it helps us plan the future!

- Azure is a pay-as-you-go platform. Having just invested a great deal into an ERP implementation, management is reluctant to invest in additional hardware and software licenses at this time. The monthly fees fit our revenue structure better.

Integrating application with cloud features

Now it's time to pull this all together, matching our application requirements to the different features of Microsoft Azure. Not every feature of Azure will be used in this project, but as we gain familiarity with Azure, we'll discuss the major features so that we can be prepared for future projects.

Requirement	Azure feature	Summary
Development environment	Development Fabric	The Azure SDK includes the Development Fabric, which we will use to develop our application.
Portal data storage	SQL Azure	An almost feature complete version of SQL Server 2008, SQL Azure will be familiar to us.
Data transfer	SSIS	SQL Server 2008 R2 supports connections to SQL Azure.
Photo upload	Blob storage, Client Library	We'll develop a simple Windows Forms Application to upload photos into blobs using a client library, rather than the REST API.
Customer portal UI	Web role	Our portal will be a custom-built ASP.NET application.
Limiting access to users	Access Control	One of AppFabric's two components is a claims-based identity service known as Access Control.
Copies of orders	SSRS	The full SSRS server is not yet supported, but we can use a local report and the ReportViewerControl.

Requirement	Azure feature	Summary
Delivery acceptance	Web role/WCF, Queue, REST API	We'll develop a simple Windows Forms application that creates a message in the queue via the REST API when a customer accepts delivery of their RV.
Processing delivery acceptance	Worker role	A worker role process will read acceptances from the queue and update the database accordingly.
Debug mode	Diagnostics	Using a value in a configuration file, the portal can be placed in a debug mode, where we can trace events. We'll retrieve logged events from Table Storage.

To sum it all up, our application will look like the following diagram:

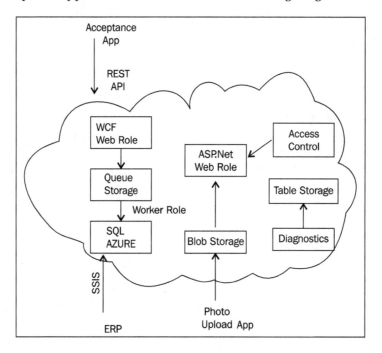

As we work through our sample application, it's important to note that this is all sample code. As with all sample applications, there are a lot of shortcuts in the code that will be taken throughout the book from this point forward. Much of the code will be used as example only, with no error handling and very little security measures. With that said, this code should not be used in any production environment unless security and error handling are added. Any code herein should also be modified to comply with coding standards, as applicable.

Creating an Azure account

A **Windows Live ID (WLID)** is necessary for creating an Azure account. Any e-mail address can be used to create a WLID so that we're free to use our corporate e-mail addresses. The account should be chosen with care, as only one ID can be used as the Account Administrator. The Account Administrator is responsible for the billing account and adding services. The login credentials will need to be shared if there are to be multiple people responsible for overall management of the Azure account, or at least being a backup administrator. Different WLIDs can be designated as Service Administrators. Service Administrators are responsible for the management of the services they've been assigned to. These tasks can include scaling the instances of our web role or adding additional table or queue storage.

Limiting the administration task to a single user isn't out of the ordinary. Usually the ultimate responsibility for production deployment should rest with one person such as the build master or equivalent role; however, for disaster planning, there should always be a capable backup in place. A management API exists and its likely management tools will be developed as time goes on. Also, MSDN Premium and higher subscriptions include Azure benefits. This is a great way to do some prototyping and testing, but the login is bound to the same one used for the MSDN account. However, this means that a new account, bound to a different e-mail address, needs to be created for the production account.

The first step in creating an Azure account is to visit `http://www.microsoft.com/windowsazure/` and choose our pricing plan. (At the time of writing, one had to click the **Sign up now** button to work on pricing plan.) These plans are likely to change over time, but they come in essentially two versions — pay-as-you-go where we are billed monthly for the services we use, and pre-paid style where we pay up front for the services we expect to use. The services in the pre-paid plans are discounted from the pay-as-you-go plan, but require a large up-front payment. If we use less than the resources we estimated, this indicates we have overpaid, but if we use more than we estimated, we need to pay for the additional services. Because estimating usage is difficult until we've been online for a while, the pay-as-you-go plan is a little easier to get started on. Once the site is up and running, we can analyze our usage and change the billing plan if necessary.

> **Windows Azure Platform Consumption**
>
> This offer is a "Pay As You Go" pricing plan that includes compute hours, storage, data transfers, SQL Azure databases and AppFabric Service Bus connections and Access Control transactions.
>
> Buy
>
> Details

Once we've found the plan that fits our needs, we click the **Buy** button, and we're taken to the **Microsoft Online Services Customer Portal** (**MOCP**). If we aren't signed in to our WLID, we're prompted to do so. The MOCP is the portal where we'll review our Azure billing, but this is not the portal where we actually manage Azure. Microsoft's other services, such as Hosted Exchange and Live Meeting, are also billed through the MOCP.

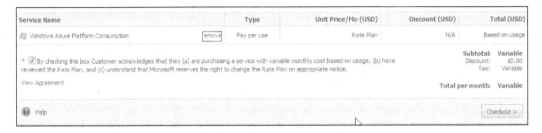

In the MOCP, we progress through a shopping cart where we supply our billing information and accept Microsoft's terms and conditions. Once we've completed our purchase, our Azure account will be provisioned and a welcome e-mail will be sent to the account's e-mail address. Now we can log in to the Windows Azure Platform Portal at `http://windows.azure.com/`, and set up the services we need. Setting up the services is a bridge we'll cross when we get there. In the meantime, we have plenty to do to get this project started. As the database is a foundation, we'll start there in the next chapter.

Summary

In this chapter, we outlined the business requirements for our portal project, matched the requirements to Azure features, and set up our Azure account. In the following chapter, we are going to take a closer look at SQL Azure. In addition to learning what SQL Azure is (and is not), we'll set up our local and portal databases.

5
Introduction to SQL Azure

Originally named SQL Data Services, SQL Azure is a feature of the Azure platform that generates a great deal of excitement. It's no overstatement to say nearly every enterprise application has a need for a relational database, and one of the leading databases utilized for enterprise applications is SQL Server. SQL Azure brings SQL Server to the cloud.

For our sample application, we'll use a simple relational database built on SQL Azure. Here's what we'll cover in this chapter:

- An in-depth look at SQL Azure
- Provisioning our SQL Azure server
- Developing and deploying our database to the cloud

Overview of SQL Azure

The first question usually asked about SQL Azure is: "Is SQL Azure really SQL Server 2008, or is it something else?" The answer is a little of both. Retail editions of SQL Server 2008 include Web, Workgroup, Standard, Enterprise, and Datacenter. SQL Azure is another edition of SQL Server 2008, and shares many of the same features as the other editions.

Development on SQL Azure is nearly identical to developing on SQL Server, with most commands and objects either fully or partially supported. However, because SQL Azure is a service, there are significant differences in how SQL Azure and on premises SQL Server are managed. At the time of writing, additional components such as **SQL Server Reporting Services (SSRS)** and **SQL Server Analysis Services (SSAS)** are not supported on SQL Azure, although on premises installations of SSRS and SSAS can consume data from SQL Azure databases. SQL Azure Reporting was announced at PDC '10, and is expected to be available in 2011.

Replication is not available in SQL Azure (don't panic, our SQL Azure databases are maintained behind the scenes in multiple copies, with automatic failover). Service Broker is another SQL Server feature currently not supported by SQL Azure. Depending on the needs of the application, a queue and worker role may be able to replace the Service Broker. Microsoft promises to introduce additional SQL Azure services soon, so we may one day see these missing features in the cloud.

SQL Azure can be used individually or in conjunction with other Azure services. In either case, local applications can connect directly to SQL Azure. When used in conjunction with Windows Azure services, local applications can also access data stored in SQL Azure via web services.

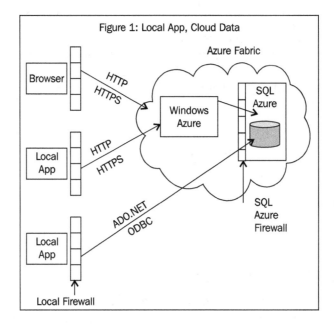

Perhaps the most common method for accessing data in SQL Azure is to use a Windows Azure Web Role or Worker Role. Using a Web Role is similar to an ASP.NET website backed by SQL Server.

Microsoft touts five key benefits in using SQL Azure:

- Manageability
- High availability
- Scalability
- A relational data model
- A familiar development model

We'll use these five benefits as the outline for our overview of SQL Azure.

Manageability

The biggest differences in managing SQL Azure and an on premise SQL Server is that we no longer have to purchase or maintain physical hardware. By design, Microsoft has separated the physical administration tasks from the logical administration tasks, and assumes responsibility for the physical management of SQL Azure. As Microsoft describes it (`http://msdn.microsoft.com/en-us/library/ee336241.aspx`):

> *[t]his approach helps SQL Azure provide a large-scale multi-tenant database service that offers enterprise-class availability, scalability, security, and self-healing.*

Microsoft has also removed the ability to control physical resources of SQL Azure. For example, there is no option to change either the hard drive or file group in which a database resides. This makes sense, as the file system is not accessible to us. Likewise, the backup and restore options are also not available (don't panic, refer to the *High availability* section later in the chapter for information regarding data protection). Likewise, there is no option to attach a database in SQL Azure.

As Azure has its own methods of load balancing and resource governing, the new Resource Governor is blocked, as are any T-SQL or DDL statements that modify or access the physical resources.

On the downside, a couple of very powerful tools we've come to rely upon are not available. Neither SQL trace flags nor the Database Tuning Advisor are available to us, which will make debugging and performance tuning more complicated.

Managing SQL Azure

SQL Azure databases are managed through the SQL Azure portal, which is part of the same portal as other Azure services, if we're using any. We use the portal to create or delete databases, and to manage database level security, but we use other tools to manage the contents of each database.

Similarities

Each SQL Azure account is provided a single instance of SQL Azure, which can contain multiple databases.

As in SQL Server 2008, we administer our databases, as well as the roles and user accounts. All connections to SQL Azure run through port 1433, same as SQL Server. If an on premise client application needs to connect directly to SQL Azure, firewalls on both ends need to have port 1433 opened. By default, external connections to a SQL Azure instance are blocked for security reasons. In order for our applications or management tools to connect to SQL Azure, we must whitelist certain IP ranges using the SQL Azure portal.

Differences

Most system-stored procedures are not supported (`http://msdn.microsoft.com/en-us/library/ee336237.aspx`), no system tables are supported, and SQL Azure has limited support for system views (`http://msdn.microsoft.com/en-us/library/ee336238.aspx`).

Databases are sold in two editions — a Web Edition, which has a maximum size of 5 GB, and a Business Edition, which has a maximum size of 50 GB. As we can expect, pricing is a tiered structure based on database size; the current pricing can be found at `http://www.microsoft.com/windowsazure/pricing/`. Security administration such as creating users and allowing access to databases is handled in the SQL Azure portal. As Microsoft handles the entire infrastructure, patches and service packs are no longer a part of our lives; nor are log files filling up drive space, as logs are not counted as part of the space calculation. However, it is possible a service pack upgrade could break some production code, and this is one of the criticisms levelled at SQL Azure by career database administrators (DBAs). Several noted DBAs discuss their concerns (`http://www.sqlmag.com/article/services/considering-sql-azure.aspx`), notably:

- The lack of a backup option prevents restoring the database to a previous time. If someone accidentally deletes a table, there is no way to retrieve it.

- Some of the more useful system stored procedures are not available, which can make troubleshooting more complicated.

The data are stored on hardware in a network that is physically out of the DBA's control. DBAs are tasked with keeping data safe and secure, and often that involves direct administration of the physical servers and working closely with network managers. With SQL Azure, uptime and security are the responsibility of a faceless group of people, and DBAs are reluctant to make guarantees about anything they cannot control.

Although there is not a true backup option, SQL Azure supports a database copy functionality, not surprisingly named SQL Azure Database Copy. The database can be copied to the same Azure server, or a different Azure server, and the copy can be scheduled. Documentation about the database copy functionality can be found at `http://msdn.microsoft.com/en-us/library/ff951624.aspx`.

The SQL Azure team addressed the issue of patching SQL Azure in a blog post at `http://blogs.msdn.com/b/sqlazure/archive/2010/04/30/10004818.aspx`. As SQL Azure keeps three redundant copies of our data on three separate instances, and only a single instance would be patched at one time, failover and redundancy are still in place during an update.

SQL Server Management Studio 2008 R2 supports direct connections to SQL Azure, but because connections to SQL Azure are solely on port 1433, the SQL Browser is not available.

High availability

Another feature of SQL Server missing in SQL Azure is replication. Without the options for backup/restore or replication, how can our data be highly available? Two concepts that we hear most often with regards to SQL Azure are "built-in data protection" and "self healing".

- **Built-in data protection**: The built-in data protection involves our data being replicated immediately and automatically across several physical machines. This replication is part of the SQL Azure platform, and we needn't set it up, neither do we have any control over it. Note that this is not the same replication as SQL Server Replication, but is a different mechanism for duplicating our data.

- **Self healing**: SQL Azure is self healing in that if a physical machine should become unavailable, there is automatic failover to another machine containing all of our data. As this failover machine is also in the Azure Fabric, the failover process is invisible to clients and no reconfiguration is necessary should a secondary machine come online.

Having high availability does not mean we can be reckless with resource utilization, and we cannot assume a connection will always remain open. In order to be fair to all tenants of SQL Azure, a SQL Azure connection may be closed for a number of reasons, including the following:

- Excessive resource utilization
- Long-running queries
- Long-running transactions

- Connections being left idle for a longer duration
- Server failures and the resulting failover

As developers, we cannot assume our connection will always be open, and we'll need to compensate accordingly.

Another way that our data are highly available is due to the scalability aspects of SQL Azure.

Scalability

Should our applications become an overnight sensation, we can add additional storage capacity via the SQL Azure portal. Database capacity can be increased on the fly, up to the subscription limits. For example, a Web Edition database comes in two sizes—1 GB and a 5 GB. For a new site, a database of the size 1 GB is more than sufficient and it also has less cost per month compared to the 5 GB database. As demands grow, we can upgrade to the 5 GB database, by simply using the ALTER DATABASE command to increase the maximum database size.

The load balancing aspects of the Azure Fabric help ensure client requests are answered and met in a timely fashion.

Relational data model

Windows Azure tables and blobs are useful, but they'll only get us so far with a complex data-driven application. For one of these, we need to rely on a relational database provider; SQL Azure is a true RDBMS in the cloud.

Familiar development model

SQL Azure is based on SQL Server—need we say more? Actually, yes, a lot more. To start with, SQL Azure supports T-SQL and returns a tabular data stream, the same as SQL Server; so, in many cases, only the connection string needs to be changed (after the database is deployed, of course). We can connect our applications to SQL Azure using familiar drivers, including System.Data.SqlClient, SQL Server 2008 and 2008 R2 ODBC Drivers, and SQL Server 2008 PHP driver (OLEDB is not supported, which is a consideration when using SSIS). Tools we can connect with include SQL Server 2008 R2 Management Studio, SQLCMD, Visual Studio 2010, and a number of third-party tools. To transfer data to SQL Azure, we can use SQL Server Integration Services (SSIS), BCP.exe, System.Data.SqlClient.SqlBulkCopy, or INSERT statements.

If we don't want to utilize direct connections to the database, we can instead use ADO.NET, ASP.NET, or ADO.NET Data Services in our applications to access data in SQL Azure.

Important to realize in this discussion is the term "familiar", rather than "identical". Because SQL Azure is a managed service, some management features have had functionality reduced or have been removed completely. T-SQL is the query language used by SQL Azure, but there are three levels of support for T-SQL commands—complete, partial, and unsupported. Further details on T-SQL support can be found at `http://msdn.microsoft.com/en-us/library/ee336250.aspx`. As we discuss similarities and differences, the discussion of differences is going to seem to outweigh the similarities. We don't need an in-depth discussion on similarities, as these should be familiar concepts and tools. Keep in mind the discussion is comparing SQL Azure and SQL Server 2008.

What's the same in SQL Azure?

One of Microsoft's goals in creating SQL Azure was to provide an environment for experienced SQL Server developers to utilize their skills. Here, we review where SQL Azure is similar to what we already know about it.

Data types

Nearly all data types are supported, including XML and geography. For a table of supported data types, visit `http://msdn.microsoft.com/en-us/library/ee336233.aspx`. The addition of the geographic and geometric data type around the MIX10 timeline raised hopes that the .NET CLR will be supported, as these data types rely on the CLR.

Database objects

As we'd expect, database tables are the same (with one exception, refer to the *What's different...* section later in the chapter), including table variables and local temporary tables. Supported table features include:

- Constants
- Constraints
- Triggers
- Statistics management
- Index creation and maintenance

SQL Azure also fully supports views, stored procedures, and user-defined functions.

Fully supported T-SQL commands

For a complete overview of supported T-SQL commands, refer to the MSDN documentation at http://msdn.microsoft.com/en-us/library/ee336270. aspx. Some of the most common T-SQL commands supported by SQL Azure are mentioned next, but this is not the complete list.

- **Data Definition Language (DDL) commands:**
  - ° Alter Role/Schema/View
  - ° Create Role/Schema/Statistics/View
  - ° Drop Login/Role/Procedure/Schema/Statistics/Synonym/ Type/User/View
  - ° DBCC SHOW_STATISTICS
  - ° UPDATE STATISTICS
- **Data Manipulation Language (DML) commands:**

Select clause/@local_variable	From
Begin_Transaction	Group By
Begin...End	Having
Cast	Order By
Convert	Top
Ceiling	Try...Catch
Coalesce	Where
Delete	Commit/Rollback/Save Transaction
Declare Cursor	While
Delete	
Truncate Table	
If...Else	

- **Data Control Language (DCL) commands**
  - ° Deny Object/Schema Permissions
  - ° Grant Object/Schema Permissions
  - ° Revoke Object/Schema Permissions

Partially supported T-SQL commands

Partial support for T-SQL commands indicates that the SQL Azure syntax does not support all the arguments or options that the SQL Server 2008 syntax does. For instance, CREATE TABLE in SQL Server 2008 has a parameter to choose the filegroup (usually ON PRIMARY); because filegroups are not selectable in SQL Azure, the filegroup argument is not supported. There are additional options not supported by the SQL Azure version of CREATE TABLE, and the official MSDN documentation should be consulted if there are questions about the support for a particular command.

The following table summarizes some of the more common T-SQL commands with partial support in SQL Azure. For the complete list of partially supported T-SQL commands, read the MSDN article at `http://msdn.microsoft.com/en-us/library/ee336267.aspx`.

Create/Alter Function	Grant/Deny/Revoke Database Permissions
Create/Alter/Drop Index	Execute
Create/Alter/Drop Table	Create/Alter User
Create/Alter/Drop Trigger	Alter Login
Create/Alter View	Enable/Disable Trigger

SQL Server built-in functions

As with T-SQL commands, the intrinsic functions of SQL Server 2008 have varying degrees of support in SQL Azure. For full details regarding SQL Azure support of SQL Server 2008 intrinsic functions, consult the official MSDN documentation at `http://msdn.microsoft.com/en-us/library/ee336248.aspx`.

Function type	Support	Examples of supported statements
Aggregate	Full	AVG, COUNT, MAX, MIN, SUM
Ranking	Full	DENSE_RANK, NTILE, RANK, ROW_NUMBER
Configuration	Partial	@@LOCK_TIMEOUT, @@SERVERNAME, @@SPID
Cursor	Full	@@CURSOR_ROWS, @@FETCH_STATUS, CURSOR_STATUS
Date and Time	Full	DATEADD, DATEDIFF, DATEPART, GETDATE, DAY, MONTH, YEAR
Mathematical	Full	ABS, CEILING, FLOOR, LOG, ROUND, SQUARE
Metadata	Partial	COL_LENGTH, COL_NAME, INDEX_COL, OBJECT_NAME
Security	Partial	CURRENT_USER, SESSION_USER, USER_NAME

Function type	Support	Examples of supported statements
String	Full	CHAR, LEFT, LEN, LTRIM, RIGHT, RTRIM
System	Partial	APP_NAME, CASE, CAST, CONVERT, COALESCE, @@IDENTITIY, ISDATE, ISNULL, @@ROWCOUNT
Text/Image	Partial	PATINDEX
ODBC String	Full	BIT_LENGTH, CONCAT
ODBC Numeric	Full	TRUNCATE
ODBC Date/Time	Full	CURRENT_DATE, CURRENT_TIME, DAYNAME, HOUR, MINUTE, QUARTER

Multiple active result sets

First introduced with ADO.NET 2.0 and SQL Server 2005, **multiple active result sets (MARS)** is the ability for multiple commands to be executed against a single connection, and to maintain multiple open recordsets. MARS can improve application performance by not limiting applications to a single command or result set.

What's different in SQL Azure?

It might seem there are more differences than similarities between SQL Server 2008 and SQL Azure, but features that are the same don't merit much discussion. In many cases, differences between SQL Azure and SQL Server 2008 are due to SQL Azure being a managed service, and much of the administration has been abstracted away from us.

One of the first differences is that we cannot choose the file placement of the database files (neither data nor log). We have no way to manage filegroups, so those options are also not available to us.

Another difference at the server level is how we set collation. Collation cannot be set at the server or database level; instead, collation can only be set at the column or expression level. The default collation for SQL Azure is SQL_LATIN1_GENERAL_CP1_CI_AS, which is a fairly general collation for US-based applications. The following is the deciphered collation:

- LATIN1_GENERAL = US English
- CP1 = code page 1252
- CI = case-insensitive
- AS = accent-sensitive

If a feature was deprecated in SQL Server 2008, SQL Azure does not support that feature. One such feature is SQL Server trace flags, which were used for debugging performance issues. SQL Azure does not support SQL trace flags.

In a major departure from SQL Server 2008, SQL Azure does not support the **Common Language Runtime (CLR)**. We also can't access server configuration options, as some don't exist and others are the responsibility of Microsoft. Additionally, SQL Azure does not support any of the SQL Server 2008 system tables.

At the database level, SQL Azure does not support database mirroring. There is no need for this, as our data are replicated across multiple physical servers.

Number of databases

When we establish a SQL Azure account, a SQL Azure instance is provisioned for us. Each SQL Azure instance can contain up to 150 databases, including the master database. Additional databases will require a separate SQL Azure instance.

Database objects

There is one difference regarding tables. Database tables must have a clustered index created before we can insert data. It is possible to create a table without a clustered index, but no inserts can be made until such an index is added. Global temporary tables are not supported in SQL Azure.

Service Broker, SQL Browser, and DTC

The *SQL Server Service Broker* handles request queuing and asynchronous messaging in a local installation of SQL Server. In SQL Azure, some of this functionality is redundant with the Azure Fabric, and hence there is no Service Broker in SQL Azure.

The *SQL Browser* is also not available in SQL Azure. The only port we can access SQL Azure through is 1433, and the SQL Browser relies on dynamic ports.

Finally, SQL Azure does not support either distributed queries or transactions, and there is no **Distributed Transaction Coordinator (DTC)**. All transactions must be local.

T-SQL commands

SQL Azure does not support the USE command for changing databases. If we're running a long set of commands and need to switch databases, we can't in SQL Azure. Instead, we must create a connection to each database, and execute the commands against the desired connection.

Also, 4-identifier referencing (`<database_name>.<schema>.<table_name>.<column>`) is not supported.

The majority of the unsupported T-SQL commands are system administration commands, which don't apply to us. Notably, most of the DBCC commands are not supported, nor are most of the ALTER commands related to databases and servers. The table that follows is a partial list of some common T-SQL commands that are unsupported; for the complete list of unsupported commands, consult the MSDN documentation at http://msdn.microsoft.com/en-us/library/ee336253.aspx.

ALTER DATABASE	GRANT/REVOKE/DENY Server Permissions
BACKUP	KILL
BULK INSERT	OPENROWSET
CREATE/ALTER/DROP LOGIN	RESTORE
DBCC CHECKDB	SELECT INTO Clause
DBCC DBREINDEX	SET ANSI_NULLS
DBCC INDEXDEFRAG	SET ANSI_PADDING_OFF
DBCC SHRINKDATABASE	WRITETEXT

System functions

A number of system functions are also not supported by SQL Azure as they could compromise information abstracted from us. Again, the following table is a partial list; the complete list of unsupported system functions is in the MSDN documentation at http://msdn.microsoft.com/en-us/library/ee336253.aspx.

fn_get_audit_file	sys.login_token
fn_get_sql	sys.user_token
sys.fn_validate_plan_guide	sys.numbered_procedure_parameters

Data synchronization

We do not have the option of replication or transaction log shipping in SQL Azure, but there is a data synchronization service currently in CTP. Utilizing the Microsoft Sync Framework, we can perform one-way or bidirectional synchronization between a number of SQL Azure databases, set up in a hub-and-spoke arrangement (rather than a true replication). When we set up synchronization, we choose a hub database to be our master database, and then pair with our member databases. Synchronization can be the entire database, or limited to a selected group of tables. Synchronization can be on demand or scheduled. Foreign key constraints are not enforced in the member databases so that data can be inserted in any order. If a foreign key relationship is necessary for our application, the member databases would not be suitable for using as a back-end database.

On the first synchronization, the database schema will be created for us in the member databases, and data will be completely synchronized. After the initial synchronization, only modified data will be synchronized. Unfortunately, schema changes will not be synchronized after the initial synchronization—we'll have to remove the synchronization, modify our database, then modify the hub database, re-establish the synchronization pairings, and start the process all over again. Member databases will be reallocated as if we were performing an initial synchronization.

An introduction to the data sync service can be found at `http://blogs.msdn.com/ b/sqlazure/archive/2010/07/06/10035099.aspx`. Because this service is in CTP at the time of writing, we recommend reviewing additional information that may have been published later for the most up-to-date information.

Security

Because SQL Azure is implemented in a different way compared to on premise SQL Server, there are a number of differences regarding security. A complete overview of SQL Azure security is found in the MSDN documentation, available at `http://msdn.microsoft.com/en-us/library/ee336235.aspx`.

First and foremost, only SQL Authentication can be used. This make sense, as there really is no Azure Active Directory a user account could be part of. Each time a connection is made, the SQL credentials must be supplied.

In SQL Azure, there is no "sa" account. Instead, the user account used to provision the instance becomes the equivalent of "sa". In SQL Server 2008, the roles *securityadmin* and *dbcreator* are both server-level roles, and are not present in SQL Azure—*loginmanager* replaces *securityadmin*, whereas *dbmanager* replaces *dbcreator*.

For security reasons, several user names are "reserved". We cannot create user names that begin with:

- Admin
- Administrator
- guest
- root
- sa

Connecting to SQL Azure is slightly different too. Encryption must always be supported, and only TCP/IP connections can be made. Before we connect to SQL Azure, the SQL Azure firewall needs an exception for our IP range, and the local computer may need a firewall exception for port 1433. If we are allowing Windows Azure applications to connect to SQL Azure, we need to whitelist Windows Azure by adding the IP address 0.0.0.0 to the Azure firewall.

Development considerations

In ADO.NET, application should have retry logic to catch errors due to service closing. Because of failover and load balancing, we can't guarantee that a connection will always be available or even accessible.

Depending on how an application supports the tabular data stream (TDS), the login name in the connection string may need to be `<login>@<server>`.

All design and user administration must be performed using T-SQL scripts. This means if we're used to performing these functions via the GUI in SSMS, it's time to brush up on the command syntax.

Finally, there are two sizes of SQL Azure database. If our database reaches its maximum size, we'll receive the **40544** error code and we'll be unable to insert/update data (but read operations will continue as normal). We'll also be unable to create new database objects.

Managing maximum size

If we reach the maximum size limit set for a Web Edition database (5 GB), then it is not easy to migrate from a Web Edition database to a Business Edition database. If our database exceeds 5 GB in size and we want to allow further growth, we would need to create a Business Edition database and use the database copy to migrate our data. We can also remove data to free some space, but there can be a 15-minute delay before more data can be inserted.

If we reach the maximum size limit set for a Business Edition database (50 GB), our only option is to remove some data to free some space. Again, there can be a 15-minute delay before more data can be inserted.

To prevent issues in our live databases, it's important we have a good policy regarding data retention and storage. Instead of storing images and other binary objects in SQL Azure, use blob service and store a pointer in the database. Older data can be archived into other SQL Azure databases, or into an on premise database.

Management tools

As we've mentioned in this chapter, developers who are used to the GUI interface of SSMS, will find managing SQL Azure frustrating. A good grasp of DDL query commands is necessary to fully manage a SQL Azure database. Sometimes, creating and managing a SQL Azure database may involve two or more tools.

SQL Azure portal

The SQL Azure portal is the only place where databases can be created and firewall rules can be set. We can also retrieve connection strings from the SQL Azure portal.

SSMS 2008 R2

Because SQL Azure was released after SQL Server 2008, SQL Server Management Studio Express 2008 R2 or any higher version must be used to connect to SQL Azure. Only the client tools need to be installed, but this will upgrade any client tools and drivers currently installed on the system.

Unlike SQL Server, tables in SQL Azure cannot be created using the properties grid style of table designer. Instead, every configuration must be performed via SQL queries. And we do mean *everything* — table creation, user creation, user permissions, setting foreign keys, and so on.

Project Houston

Project Houston is a Silverlight-based database editing tool provided by Microsoft. It can be found at http://www.sqlazurelabs.com/houston.aspx. At the time of writing, Project Houston was in CTP 1. Databases must be created in the SQL Azure portal; however, in Houston we can create tables using the more familiar properties grid. At the time of writing, alterations to tables (such as adding foreign keys) must still be done with DDL queries. We can also run queries, create stored procedures and views, and directly enter/edit data. Creating a new table is shown in the following screenshot:

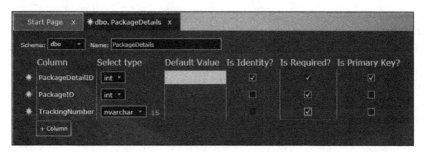

One advantage of using Houston over SSMS is that we don't need to configure firewall rules for every client location. Because Houston is a Microsoft service, the 0.0.0.0 rule allows access to our databases.

Access 2010

In an announcement that made a great number of enterprise developers weep, Microsoft added support for SQL Azure to Access 2010 via ODBC. Tables can be linked or users can use pass-through queries. Access 2010 support provides a database entry point business users are familiar with, but which can sometimes grow into an unmanageable mess.

The SQL Server Native Client 10.0 or higher is required for access to connect to SQL Azure. This driver is installed with any flavor of SQL Server 2008 R2, SSMS 2008 R2, or as a standalone driver in the SQL Server 2008 R2 Feature Pack at `http://www.microsoft.com/downloads/en/details.aspx?FamilyID=ceb4346f-657f-4d28-83f5-aae0c5c83d52&displaylang=en`.

If we want to migrate an existing Access 2010 database to SQL Azure, the recommendation is to use the SQL Server Migration Assistant (SSMA) rather than the Upsizing Wizard.

Managing databases, logins, and roles in SQL Azure

Managing databases and logins in SQL Azure is very similar to managing them in an on-site instance of SQL Server. Using T-SQL commands, you can create/alter/drop logins, create/drop databases, and create/alter/drop users, though some parameters are not supported. One thing to remember is that all server-level and database-level security must be applied to the "master" database that is created when your SQL Azure service has been provisioned. Also, the administrator username you selected when provisioning the service is similar to the "sa" user in an on-site instance of SQL Server.

There are also two new roles in SQL Azure: **loginmanager** and **dbmanager**. The *loginmanager* role is similar to the *securityadmin* role of SQL Server, whereas the *dbmanager* role is similar to the dbcreator role of SQL Server. You can add users to either of these roles if you want them to have the permissions to create/alter/drop logins and users (loginmanager), or create/alter/drop databases (dbmanager).

Migrating schema and data

The ability to create new database objects is good, but for a number of applications we'll need to migrate an existing database. For an on-premise SQL Server, to move a database, we'd commonly use a backup and restore, or detach and reattach—neither of those options are available to us in SQL Azure. However, many of the other options we might use, such as DAC Packs or SSIS, are available to us in Azure. An overview of how to migrate applications and data to SQL Azure can be found at `http://msdn.microsoft.com/en-us/library/ee730904.aspx`.

Manually scripting objects and data

Before any scripts are manually created, there are a few scripting options we need to change to ensure our objects are created correctly on SQL Azure. In SSMS, the settings we need to change can be found at **Tools | Options | SQL Server Object Explorer | Scripting**. The first setting we need to change is, setting the **Script for database engine type** option to the **SQL Azure Database** option, as seen in the following screenshot. Changing this setting will change some other settings and disable others.

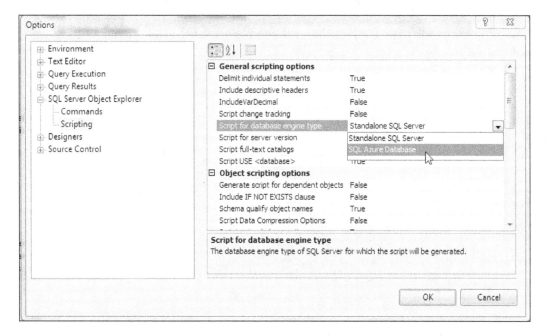

By default, dependent objects will not be scripted. This may need to be set to "True" depending on the needs and database schema. Likewise, triggers and indices will not be scripted by default. If these are necessary, we need to enable these settings too.

For complete control over the migration process, we can create scripts for specific objects and data by using SSMS, then running these scripts into our SQL Azure database. For large databases, this can be a time-consuming process. Using this method will script foreign keys, so it may be necessary to create tables in a particular order, or tweak the scripts to run table first, and then defaults and foreign keys.

A related option is to use the **Generate Script Wizard (GSW)**. To use the GSW, right-click on the database name and choose **Tasks | Generate Scripts**. The table scripts are not created in a relational manner, so we need to ensure we run the scripts in the proper order. The output is a `.sql` file, which we can execute against a database instance.

SQL Azure Migration Wizard

The SQL Azure Migration Wizard is a community project that can be used to migrate objects and data from SQL Server 2005/2008 databases. The project can be found at `http://sqlazuremw.codeplex.com/`. Because there may be incompatibilities between the older SQL Server versions and SQL Azure, it is recommended that a test migration be performed into a local SQL Server 2008 (or higher) database, and then migrated into SQL Azure.

The SQL Azure Migration Wizard allows us to migrate an entire database, or to select specific objects to migrate, as seen in the next screenshot. The output is T-SQL scripts that can be executed in SQL Azure to make the necessary changes.

We have a great deal of control over the migration settings, including migrating only tables, only data, or tables and data by changing the **Script Table / Data** setting. It's a good idea to fully review these setting before generating the SQL scripts.

SQL Server Integration Services (SSIS)

We can migrate tables and data using the SQL Server Import and Export Wizard, or create an SSIS package from scratch. SSIS packages do not execute on SQL Azure, they can only create connections to SQL Azure database and perform the functions as programmed. If we plan on using SSIS, we will need an on-premise SQL Server instance to host the packages.

SQL Server Import and Export Wizard

The SQL Server Import and Export Wizard (http://msdn.microsoft.com/en-us/library/ms140052.aspx) can be used to migrate tables and data between an on-premises SQL Server and SQL Azure. At the end of the wizard, we have the option of saving the package created by the wizard so that we can use it again. To launch the wizard, right-click on a database in an on-premise instance and choose **Tasks | Export Data** (at the time of writing, the Import wizard cannot be launched by clicking on a SQL Azure database, so we have to export from our on-premise instance).

We can choose to migrate all the data in one or more tables, or write a query to migrate a limited data set from a single table, as seen in the next screenshot:

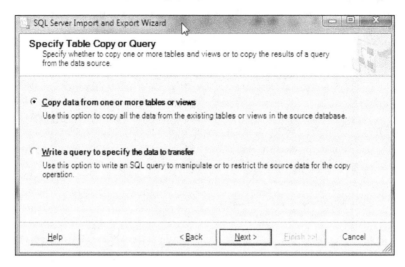

We can also set options to create tables, enable identity insert, and more, by choosing the **Edit Mappings** button from the **Select Source Tables and Views** screen. These are important options to consider if we want to save the package produced by the wizard.

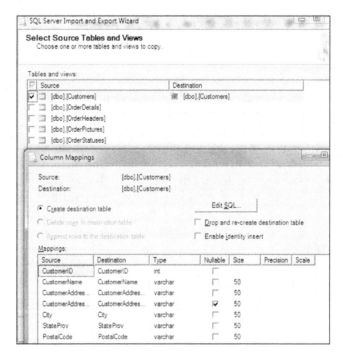

Although views can be selected, the view definition is not migrated. The view is treated as a table in the source database, and a table will be created in the target database with the same name as the view, containing the data in the view at the time the package was run. View definitions should be migrated with some other technique to ensure they are migrated correctly.

At the end of the wizard, we can choose to save the SSIS package as well as execute it. Be careful while saving the package, as everything we asked the package to do will be saved, and some of the settings we chose may be a good idea for a first time (such as creating tables) but not a subsequent run (as the tables exist, they cannot be created and the package will fail).

Creating packages from scratch

We can create SSIS packages to migrate database objects and data to SQL Azure. SSIS uses an ODBC connection to connect to SQL Azure, and just as with Access 2010, we need to make sure the SQL Server Native Client 10.0 driver is installed. Besides the driver requirement, creating an SSIS package in **Business Intelligence Development Studio (BIDS)** is the same as working with other SQL Server versions.

When running on a schedule, SSIS packages are not suitable for migrating database objects. SSIS is good for migrating data, and may be an alternative to the data synchronization services mentioned above.

DAC Packs

One more option we have is the **data-tier application package (DAC Pack)**. DAC Packs can be used to migrate database schemas from one server instance to another. DAC Packs can be created either in SSMS or with custom .NET code. The SSMS option is easier, but is a manual process. An overview of using DAC Packs can be found at http://msdn.microsoft.com/en-us/library/ee210546.aspx.

We can extract DAC Packs from SQL Server 2000 or higher, but we can deploy DAC Packs only on SQL Azure and SQL Server 2008 R2 or higher a version.

A DAC Pack is created in SSMS by right-clicking on a database name, then choosing **Tasks | Extract data-tier application**. By following through the wizard, we can create a DAC Pack. The output of the Extract wizard is a file stored on our local machine. A .dacpac file is actually just a ZIP file containing several XML files that describe our database's structure.

To deploy the DAC Pack, we need to connect to the database instance in SSMS 2008 R2, right-click on the instance name, and choose **Deploy Data-tier Application**.

One of the major downsides to a DAC Pack is that not all object types are supported. We also don't get to choose what is included in our DAC Pack; SQL Server assumes we want everything to be included. This means we need to be careful with what we're doing or we might migrate some half-baked features into production, or migrate views or stored procedures that reference a non-available database.

DAC Packs do not migrate data. So after we deploy a DAC Pack, we would need to use SSIS to migrate the data.

If we want to use custom .NET code, the MSDN documentation for the DAC Pack namespace can be found at `http://msdn.microsoft.com/en-us/library/microsoft.sqlserver.management.dac.aspx`.

BCP

For migrating large amounts of data to SQL Azure, the command line BCP.exe utility can be utilized. BCP works the same with SQL Azure as any other version of SQL Server. Documentation for the BCP.exe utility can be found at `http://msdn.microsoft.com/en-us/library/ms162802(SQL.105).aspx`.

The Jupiter Motor's ERP system database and the Dealer Orders database

Here is a visual representation of our databases. The following is the visual look at the portal database:

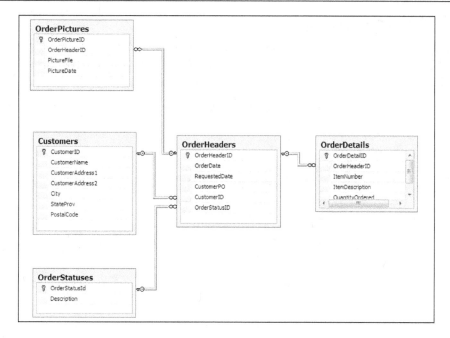

The following is the visual look of the Jupiter ERP database:

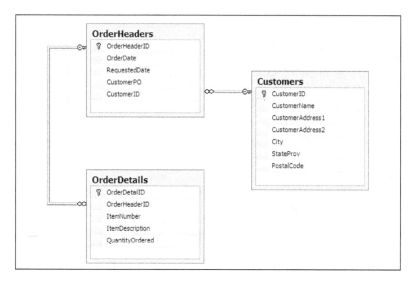

The portal database design is very simple, consisting of only five tables. The Jupiter ERP database has only three tables, and will be a local database (this will not live in SQL Azure; it is a representation of an on-site ERP system). Now that we know what the designs of the databases are, let's get started with the database creation of the portal database in SQL Azure.

SQL Azure portal

When we sign up for the SQL Azure service at `http://windows.azure.com`, we are given a URL to the Azure portal. To access our SQL Azure area of the portal, click on the link in the menu bar to the left for SQL Azure, as seen here:

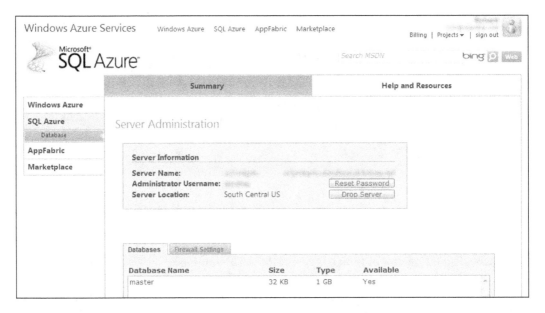

There is some basic information such as the **Server Name** (the URL is for connections from external sources, such as SSMS), the **Administrator Username**, and our selected **Server Location**, which we will use throughout our travels in SQL Azure. Also, in the box at the bottom we can see a visual list of our databases (including the default master database that was already created for us). We are also able to change firewall settings to let specific IP blocks into our SQL Azure service. We can also create a new database here, view connection strings to the selected database, test connections to the database, or drop a database.

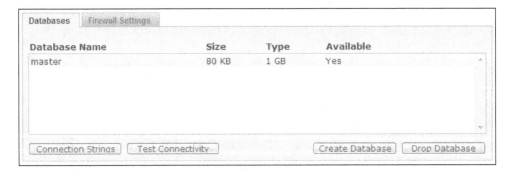

To use SQL Azure from an outside connection via a tool such as SSMS, we must whitelist the IP block we are connecting from. To do this, select the **Firewall Settings** tab and click the **Add Rule** button. A popup opens that allows us to enter IP range. To make things a little easier, our current IP address is displayed. When finished, click the **Submit** button; it may take up to five minutes for the changes to propagate.

Add Firewall Rule

Name:

IP Range:

                to

Your IP address:

Submit   Cancel

Note: Firewall rules may take up to 5 minutes before they come into effect.

Creating our database

Now that we've done everything we need to do to hit our SQL Azure database from an outside connection, let's set up the database by using the Server URL in SSMS and our Administrator Username/Password to connect from there. Once connected, the following scripts will create our application databases, add logins named `JupiterMotors` for the `JupiterERP` database and `Portal` for the `Portal` database (which we will use throughout the book), and all the tables/keys in the diagram at the beginning of the chapter. Please note that the CREATE DATABASE and CREATE LOGIN commands must be executed separately in the master database, and the CREATE USER command is to be executed in the Jupiter ERP database. Also, we must log into the each database through SSMS to run the script for creating the tables and keys.

We will first start with creating the portal database, login, and user:

```
/* Execute this line in the master database */
CREATE DATABASE [Portal]


/* Execute this line in the master database */
CREATE LOGIN Portal WITH Password='P@ssword'


/* Execute this line in the Portal database */
CREATE USER Portal FROM LOGIN Portal
```

Next, we're going to create the tables. This code must be executed after logging directly into the portal database using SSMS:

```
/*******************************************************************
*************
*   This section below will create our tables for the Portal database
*          -Customers table
*                  This table will hold all of our Customer address
information
*          -OrderStauuses table
*                  This table will hold all of our Order Statuses for
our orders
*          -OrderHeaders table
*                  This table will hold our Order Header information
*          -OrderDetails table
*                  This table will hold our Order Detail information
*          -OrderPictures table
*                  This table will hold the information of the pictures
placed into
*                  Blob Storage for the Jupiter Motors portal
*******************************************************************
*************/
SET ANSI_NULLS ON
GO
SET QUOTED_IDENTIFIER ON
GO
SET ANSI_PADDING ON
GO
CREATE TABLE [dbo].[Customers](
    [CustomerID] [int] IDENTITY(1,1) NOT NULL,
    [CustomerName] [varchar](50) NOT NULL,
    [CustomerAddress1] [varchar](50) NOT NULL,
    [CustomerAddress2] [varchar](50) NULL,
    [City] [varchar](50) NOT NULL,
    [StateProv] [varchar](50) NOT NULL,
    [PostalCode] [varchar](50) NOT NULL,
 CONSTRAINT [PK_Customers] PRIMARY KEY CLUSTERED
(
    [CustomerID] ASC
))
GO

CREATE TABLE [dbo].[OrderStatuses](
    [OrderStatusId] [int] IDENTITY(1,1) NOT NULL,
    [Description] [varchar](50) NOT NULL,
```

```
    CONSTRAINT [PK_OrderStatuses] PRIMARY KEY CLUSTERED
(
    [OrderStatusId] ASC
))
GO

CREATE TABLE [dbo].[OrderHeaders](
    [OrderHeaderID] [int] IDENTITY(1,1) NOT NULL,
    [OrderDate] [smalldatetime] NOT NULL,
    [RequestedDate] [smalldatetime] NOT NULL,
    [CustomerPO] [varchar](50) NOT NULL,
    [CustomerID] [int] NOT NULL,
    [OrderStatusID] [int] NOT NULL,
 CONSTRAINT [PK_OrderHeader] PRIMARY KEY CLUSTERED
(
    [OrderHeaderID] ASC
))
GO

CREATE TABLE [dbo].[OrderPictures](
    [OrderPictureID] [int] IDENTITY(1,1) NOT NULL,
    [OrderHeaderID] [int] NOT NULL,
    [PictureFile] [varchar](100) NOT NULL,
    [PictureDate] [smalldatetime] NOT NULL,
 CONSTRAINT [PK_OrderPictures] PRIMARY KEY CLUSTERED
(
    [OrderPictureID] ASC
))
GO

CREATE TABLE [dbo].[OrderDetails](
    [OrderDetailID] [int] IDENTITY(1,1) NOT NULL,
    [OrderHeaderID] [int] NOT NULL,
    [ItemNumber] [int] NOT NULL,
    [ItemDescription] [nchar](10) NULL,
    [QuantityOrdered] [int] NOT NULL,
 CONSTRAINT [PK_OrderDetails] PRIMARY KEY CLUSTERED
(
    [OrderDetailID] ASC
))
GO
```

After the tables have been created, let's now create the database keys:

```
/**********************************************************************
*************
*   This section below will create our foreign keys for the Portal
database
*           -FK_OrderDetails_OrderHeaders
*               Links OrderDetails to OrderHeaders using
OrderHeaderID Primary Key
*           -FK_OrderHeaders_Customers
*               Links OrderHeaders to Customers using CustomerID
Primary Key
*           -FK_OrderPictures_OrderHeaders
*               Links OrderPictures to OrderHeaders using
OrderHeaderID Primary Key
*           -FK_OrderHeaders_OrderStatuses
*               Links OrderHeaders to OrderStatuses using
OrderStatusID Primary Key
**********************************************************************
*************/
ALTER TABLE [dbo].[OrderDetails]  WITH CHECK ADD  CONSTRAINT [FK_
OrderDetails_OrderHeaders] FOREIGN KEY([OrderHeaderID])
REFERENCES [dbo].[OrderHeaders] ([OrderHeaderID])
GO
ALTER TABLE [dbo].[OrderDetails] CHECK CONSTRAINT [FK_OrderDetails_
OrderHeaders]
GO


ALTER TABLE [dbo].[OrderPictures]  WITH CHECK ADD  CONSTRAINT [FK_
OrderPictures_OrderHeaders] FOREIGN KEY([OrderHeaderID])
REFERENCES [dbo].[OrderHeaders] ([OrderHeaderID])
GO
ALTER TABLE [dbo].[OrderPictures] CHECK CONSTRAINT [FK_OrderPictures_
OrderHeaders]
GO


ALTER TABLE [dbo].[OrderHeaders]  WITH CHECK ADD  CONSTRAINT [FK_
OrderHeaders_Customers] FOREIGN KEY([CustomerID])
REFERENCES [dbo].[Customers] ([CustomerID])
GO
ALTER TABLE [dbo].[OrderHeaders] CHECK CONSTRAINT [FK_OrderHeaders_
Customers]
GO


ALTER TABLE [dbo].[OrderHeaders]  WITH CHECK ADD  CONSTRAINT [FK_
OrderHeaders_OrderStatuses] FOREIGN KEY([OrderStatusID])
```

```
REFERENCES [dbo].[OrderStatuses] ([OrderStatusId])
GO
ALTER TABLE [dbo].[OrderHeaders] CHECK CONSTRAINT [FK_OrderHeaders_
OrderStatuses]
GO
```

Finally, for our Portal database, we must create the stored procedures to insert customers, order headers, and order detail:

```
/*********************************************************************
*************
*    This section below will create our stored procedures in the
*    Portal database.  There is one stored procedure for creating
*    the new customer placing the order, one to insert the Order
Header, and one
*    that will insert each line item on the order into the Order
Details table.
*    Orders will be inserted with a OrderStatusID = 1 (Unapproved) in
the
*    OrderHeaders table.
*********************************************************************
************/
SET ANSI_NULLS ON
GO
SET QUOTED_IDENTIFIER ON
GO
CREATE PROCEDURE [dbo].[NewCustomer]
@Name varchar(50),
@Address1 varchar(50),
@Address2 varchar(50),
@City varchar(50),
@StateProv varchar(50),
@PostalCode varchar(50)
AS
BEGIN
    SET NOCOUNT ON;

    INSERT INTO Customers(CustomerName, CustomerAddress1,
CustomerAddress2, City, StateProv, PostalCode)
    VALUES(@Name, @Address1, @Address2, @City, @StateProv,
@PostalCode)

    SELECT Scope_Identity()

END
GO
```

```
CREATE PROCEDURE [dbo].[NewOrderHeader]
@OrderDate datetime,
@RequestedDate datetime,
@CustomerPO varchar(50),
@CustomerID int

AS
BEGIN
    SET NOCOUNT ON;

    INSERT INTO OrderHeaders(OrderDate, RequestedDate, CustomerPO,
       CustomerID, OrderStatusID)
    VALUES (@OrderDate, @RequestedDate, @CustomerPO, @CustomerID, 1)

    SELECT SCOPE_IDENTITY()

END
GO


CREATE PROCEDURE [dbo].[NewOrderDetail]
@OrderHeaderID int,
@ItemNumber varchar(50),
@ItemDescription varchar(50),
@QuantityOrdered int

AS
BEGIN
    SET NOCOUNT ON;

INSERT INTO OrderDetails(OrderHeaderID, ItemNumber, ItemDescription,
QuantityOrdered)
VALUES(@OrderHeaderID, @ItemNumber, @ItemDescription,
@QuantityOrdered)

END
GO
```

Our portal maintains the order status in the OrderHeaders table. Let's insert the statuses in the OrderStatuses table:

```
/****************************************************************
 *   These statements will insert the Order Statuses
 ****************************************************************/

INSERT INTO dbo.OrderStatuses(Description)
```

```
VALUES ('Unapproved')

INSERT INTO dbo.OrderStatuses(Description)
VALUES ('Approved')

INSERT INTO dbo.OrderStatuses(Description)
VALUES ('Scheduled For Production')

INSERT INTO dbo.OrderStatuses(Description)
VALUES ('In Production')

INSERT INTO dbo.OrderStatuses(Description)
VALUES ('In Transit for Delivery')

INSERT INTO dbo.OrderStatuses(Description)
VALUES ('Accepted')

INSERT INTO dbo.OrderStatuses(Description)
VALUES ('Complete')
```

That takes care of the Portal database. We will now create the JupiterERP database. This creation of database, logins, users, tables, keys, and stored procedures use the same steps as creating the Portal database above, only the database structure is much simpler and this database will reside on our physical machine. Remember that this database is stored on a local instance of SQL Server, so we have our full set of features with this database (though the scripts were written with the simplest features for ease):

```
/* Execute this line in the master database */
CREATE DATABASE [JupiterERP]


/* Execute this line in the master database */
CREATE LOGIN JupiterMotors WITH Password='P@ssword'


/* Execute this line in the JupiterERP database */
CREATE USER JupiterMotors FROM LOGIN JupiterMotors
```

The creation script for the tables and keys follows (remember to connect directly to the local instance of our JupiterERP database to run this script and the stored procedures script):

```
/***********************************************************************
*************
*   This section below will create our tables for the JupiterERP
    database
*           -Customers table
*                   This table will hold all of our Customer address
                    information
*           -OrderHeaders table
*                   This table will hold our Order Header information
*           -OrderDetails table
*                   This table will hold our Order Detail information
************************************************************************
************/

SET ANSI_NULLS ON
GO
SET QUOTED_IDENTIFIER ON
GO
SET ANSI_PADDING ON
GO
CREATE TABLE [dbo].[Customers](
    [CustomerID] [int] IDENTITY(1,1) NOT NULL,
    [CustomerName] [varchar](50) NOT NULL,
    [CustomerAddress1] [varchar](50) NOT NULL,
    [CustomerAddress2] [varchar](50) NULL,
    [City] [varchar](50) NOT NULL,
    [StateProv] [varchar](50) NOT NULL,
    [PostalCode] [varchar](50) NOT NULL,
 CONSTRAINT [PK_Customers] PRIMARY KEY CLUSTERED
(
    [CustomerID] ASC
))

CREATE TABLE [dbo].[OrderHeaders](
    [OrderHeaderID] [int] IDENTITY(1,1) NOT NULL,
    [OrderDate] [smalldatetime] NOT NULL,
    [RequestedDate] [smalldatetime] NOT NULL,
    [CustomerPO] [varchar](50) NOT NULL,
    [CustomerID] [int] NOT NULL,
 CONSTRAINT [PK_OrderHeader] PRIMARY KEY CLUSTERED
(
```

```
        [OrderHeaderID] ASC
))

CREATE TABLE [dbo].[OrderDetails](
    [OrderDetailID] [int] IDENTITY(1,1) NOT NULL,
    [OrderHeaderID] [int] NOT NULL,
    [ItemNumber] [int] NOT NULL,
    [ItemDescription] [nchar](10) NULL,
    [QuantityOrdered] [int] NOT NULL,
 CONSTRAINT [PK_OrderDetails] PRIMARY KEY CLUSTERED
(
    [OrderDetailID] ASC
))
GO


/*********************************************************************
*************
*   This section below will create our foreign keys for the JupiterERP
    database
*           -FK_OrderDetails_OrderHeaders
*               Links OrderDetails to OrderHeaders using
OrderHeaderID Primary Key
*           -FK_OrderHeaders_Customers
*               Links OrderHeaders to Customers using CustomerID
Primary Key
*********************************************************************
************/

ALTER TABLE [dbo].[OrderDetails]  WITH CHECK ADD  CONSTRAINT [FK_
OrderDetails_OrderHeaders] FOREIGN KEY([OrderHeaderID])
REFERENCES [dbo].[OrderHeaders] ([OrderHeaderID])
GO
ALTER TABLE [dbo].[OrderDetails] CHECK CONSTRAINT [FK_OrderDetails_
OrderHeaders]
GO


ALTER TABLE [dbo].[OrderHeaders]  WITH CHECK ADD  CONSTRAINT [FK_
OrderHeaders_Customers] FOREIGN KEY([CustomerID])
REFERENCES [dbo].[Customers] ([CustomerID])
GO
ALTER TABLE [dbo].[OrderHeaders] CHECK CONSTRAINT [FK_OrderHeaders_
Customers]
GO
```

The last thing to do is to create the stored procedures to add a customer, an order header, and the order detail:

```
/**************************************************************
*************
*   This section below will create our stored procedures in the
*   JupiterERP database.  There is one stored procedure for creating
*   the new customer placing the order, one to insert the Order
Header, and one
*   that will insert each line item on the order into the Order
Details table.
**************************************************************
***********/

SET ANSI_NULLS ON
GO
SET QUOTED_IDENTIFIER ON
GO
CREATE PROCEDURE [dbo].[NewCustomer]
@Name varchar(50),
@Address1 varchar(50),
@Address2 varchar(50),
@City varchar(50),
@StateProv varchar(50),
@PostalCode varchar(50)
AS
BEGIN
    SET NOCOUNT ON;

    INSERT INTO Customers(CustomerName, CustomerAddress1,
      CustomerAddress2, City, StateProv, PostalCode)
    VALUES(@Name, @Address1, @Address2, @City, @StateProv,
      @PostalCode)

    SELECT SCOPE_IDENTITY()

END
GO

CREATE PROCEDURE [dbo].[NewOrderHeader]
@OrderDate datetime,
```

```
@RequestedDate datetime,
@CustomerPO varchar(50),
@CustomerID int

AS
BEGIN
    SET NOCOUNT ON;

    INSERT INTO OrderHeaders(OrderDate, RequestedDate, CustomerPO,
      CustomerID)
    VALUES (@OrderDate, @RequestedDate, @CustomerPO, @CustomerID)

    SELECT SCOPE_IDENTITY()

END
GO


CREATE PROCEDURE [dbo].[NewOrderDetail]
@OrderHeaderID int,
@ItemNumber varchar(50),
@ItemDescription varchar(50),
@QuantityOrdered int

AS
BEGIN
    SET NOCOUNT ON;

INSERT INTO OrderDetails(OrderHeaderID, ItemNumber, ItemDescription,
QuantityOrdered)
VALUES(@OrderHeaderID, @ItemNumber, @ItemDescription,
    @QuantityOrdered)

END
GO
```

At this point, our databases have been created, our logins and users have been created, and the database tables, keys, and stored procedures exist in the databases. We're now ready for the next step!

Summary

In this chapter, we gained an overview of SQL Azure, and examined some of the similarities and differences between SQL Server 2008 and SQL Azure. We also walked through setting up our SQL Azure service. Because SQL Azure is a managed service, a number of SQL Server commands and functions are not available to us, and many of the administrative functions have also been removed. There are considerations developers and administrators alike must make when building or migrating an application to Azure. Finally, we provisioned and created our local JupiterERP database and portal database in SQL Azure.

6
Azure Blob Storage

In movie mythology, blobs are ever-growing creatures that consume everything in their path. In Azure, blobs just seem to be the same. A **blob**, or **binary large object**, is an Azure storage mechanism with both streaming and random read/write capabilities. Blob Storage is accessed via a .NET client library or a rich REST API, and libraries for a number of languages, including Ruby and PHP, are available. With the addition of the Windows Azure Content Delivery Network, blobs have become a very functional and powerful storage option.

Blobs in the Azure ecosystem

Blobs are one of the three simple storage options for Windows Azure, and are designed to store large files in binary format (refer to the Windows Azure diagram in *Chapter 2*, *The Nickel Tour of Azure*, for a reminder of how blobs fit into the Azure ecosystem). There are two types of blobs — block blobs and page blobs. **Block blobs** are designed for streaming, and each blob can have a size of up to 200 GB. **Page blobs** are designed for read/write access and each blob can store up to 1 TB each. If we're going to store images or video for use in our application, we'd store them in blobs. On our local systems, we would probably store these files in different folders. In our Azure account, we place blobs into containers, and just as a local hard drive can contain any number of folders, each Azure account can have any number of containers.

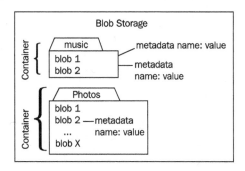

Similar to folders on a hard drive, access to blobs is set at the container level, where permissions can be either "public read" or "private". In addition to permission settings, each container can have 8 KB of metadata used to describe or categorize it (metadata are stored as name/value pairs). Each blob can be up to 1 TB depending on the type of blob, and can also have up to 8 KB of metadata. For data protection and scalability, each blob is replicated at least three times, and "hot blobs" are served from multiple servers. Even though the cloud can accept blobs of up to 1 TB in size, Development Storage can accept blobs only up to 2 GB. This typically is not an issue for development, but still something to remember when developing locally.

Page blobs form the basis for Windows Azure Drive—a service that allows Azure storage to be mounted as a local NTFS drive on the Azure instance, allowing existing applications to run in the cloud and take advantage of Azure-based storage while requiring fewer changes to adapt to the Azure environment. Azure drives are individual virtual hard drives (VHDs) that can range in size from 16 MB to 1 TB. Each Windows Azure instance can mount up to 16 Azure drives, and these drives can be mounted or dismounted dynamically. Also, Windows Azure Drive can be mounted as readable/writable from a single instance of an Azure service, or it can be mounted as a read-only drive for multiple instances. At the time of writing, there was no driver that allowed direct access to the page blobs forming Azure drives, but the page blobs can be downloaded, used locally, and uploaded again using the standard blob API.

Creating Blob Storage

Blob Storage can be used independent of other Azure services, and even if we've set up a Windows Azure or SQL Azure account, Blob Storage is not automatically created for us. To create a Blob Storage service, we need to follow these steps:

1. Log in to the Windows Azure Developer portal and select our project.

2. After we select our project, we should see the project page, as shown in the next screenshots:

3. Clicking the **New Service** link on the application page takes us to the service creation page, as shown next:

4. Selecting **Storage Account** allows us to choose a name and description for our storage service. This information is used to identify our services in menus and listings.

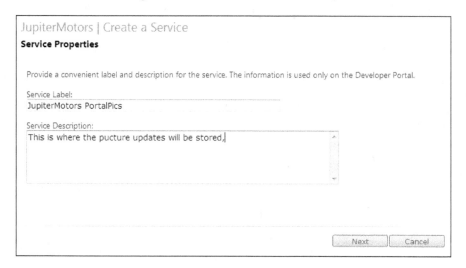

5. Next, we choose a unique name for our storage account. This name must be unique across all of Azure—it can include only lowercase letters and numbers, and must be at least three characters long.

6. If our account name is available, we then choose how to localize our data. Localization is handled by "affinity groups", which tie our storage service to the data centers in different geographic regions. For some applications, it may not matter where we locate our data. For other applications, we may want multiple affinity groups to provide timely content delivery. And for a few applications, regulatory requirements may mean we have to bind our data to a particular region.

7. Clicking the **Create** button creates our storage service, and when complete, a summary page is shown. The top half of the summary page reiterates the description of our service and provides the endpoints and 256-bit access keys. These access keys are very important—they are the authentication keys we need to pass in our request if we want to access private storage or add/update a blob.

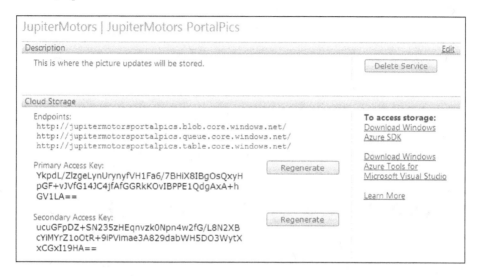

8. The bottom portion of the confirmation page reiterates the affinity group the storage service belongs to. We can also enable a content delivery network and custom domain for our Blob Storage account.

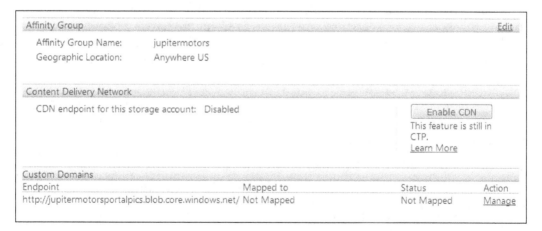

9. Once we create a service, it's shown on the portal menu and in the project summary once we select a project.

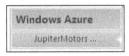

10. That's it! We now have our storage services created.

We're now ready to look at blobs in a little more depth.

Windows Azure Content Delivery Network

Delivering content worldwide can be a challenge. As more and more people gain access to the Internet, more and more people (hopefully) will be visiting our site. The ability to deliver content to our visitors is limited by the resources we've used for our application. One way of handling bottlenecks is to move commonly used files (such as CSS or JavaScript libraries) or large media files (such as photos, music, and videos) to another network with much greater bandwidth, and with multiple locations around the world. These networks are known as **Content Delivery Networks** (**CDNs**), and when properly utilized to deliver content from a node geographically closer to the requester, they can greatly speed up the delivery of our content.

The Windows Azure Content Delivery Network is a service that locates our publicly available blobs in data centers around the world, and automatically routes our users' requests to the geographically closest data center. The CDN can be enabled for any storage account, as we saw in the service setup.

To access blobs via the CDN, different URL is used than for standard access. The standard endpoint for our sample application is `http://jupitermotors.blob.core.windows.net`. When we set up CDN access, our service is assigned a GUID, and CDN access is through a generated URL, which will be assigned in our Windows Azure Developer portal when we enable the feature. A custom domain can also be used with the CDN.

Blobs are cached at the CDN endpoints for a specified amount of time (default, 72 hours). The **time-to-live** (**TTL**) is specified as the HTTP Cache-Control header. If a blob is not found at the geographically closest data center, the blob is retrieved from the main Blob Storage and cached at that data center for the specified TTL.

Blob Storage Data Model

The Blob Storage Data Model is a simple model consisting of four different components: a storage account, containers, blobs, and blocks or pages. A container is a way to organize blobs. Think of a container as a "folder" that can hold many "files". These "files" are blobs. A blob consists of one or more blocks or pages of data. In the following diagram, we can see a visual representation of a container, blobs, and blocks. Our storage account can hold an unlimited number of containers, and each container can hold an unlimited number of blobs. Each blob, as mentioned above, can be either 200 GB or smaller (block blob) or up to 1 TB (page blob). Each block in a block blob can be up to 4 MB in size, which implies that a 200 GB block blob will contain a tremendous number of blocks.

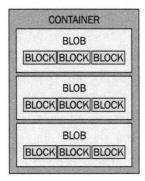

Blob Storage

There are two mechanisms for accessing Blob storage — the REST-ful Blob Storage API and a .NET client library called the StorageClient Library. Documentation for the REST-ful API can be found at `http://msdn.microsoft.com/en-us/library/dd135733.aspx`, whereas the StorageClient Library documentation can be found at `http://msdn.microsoft.com/en-us/library/ee741723.aspx`.

Representational State Transfer

What is REST? REST stands for Representational State Transfer, and even if the term is not familiar, the concepts probably are. REST architecture forms the basis for the World Wide Web. In REST, a client sends a document to a server, called as request, and the server replies with another document, called as response. Both the request and the response documents are "representations" of either the current or intended "state". The state in this context is the sum total of the information on the server. A request to list all the posts in a forum receives a response describing the current state of the forum posts. A request containing a reply to one of those posts represents the intended state, as it changes the forum's information. Systems built on these concepts and utilizing a set of HTTP verbs are described as **REST-ful**. For more information on REST, a good starting point is http://en.wikipedia.org/wiki/Representational_State_Transfer.

The Blob Storage API

Now that we have an idea of what REST is, we now understand why it's important that the Blob Storage API is built on a "RESTful" interface. The Blob Storage API uses the HTTP/REST operations PUT, GET, DELETE, and HEAD. These operations perform the following functions:

- PUT: This command will insert a new object, or if the object already exists, it will overwrite the old object with the new one.
- GET: This command will retrieve an object.
- DELETE: This command will delete an object.
- HEAD: This command will retrieve properties and metadata.

Using the Blob Storage API, we can work with containers, blobs, and blocks via HTTP/REST operations. As we examine the API in the coming sections, we will notice that many of the operator/request URI combinations are similar. The magic happens with the request headers and request bodies. In *Chapter 9, Web Role*, when we discuss the Azure web role and build the front-end application, we will take a deeper look at some of these operator/request URIs.

Working with containers using the REST interface

We are able to perform a number of actions with containers using the Blob Storage API. Containers help us to:

- List all containers for our storage account
- Create new containers
- Retrieve all container properties and metadata
- Set metadata on containers
- Get and set the access control list (ACL) for a container
- Delete a container (and its contents)

Working with containers using the StorageClient library

The CloudBlobClient class (http://msdn.microsoft.com/en-us/library/ee758637.aspx) is the class used to interact with blob containers. The CloudBlobContainer class (http://msdn.microsoft.com/en-us/library/microsoft.windowsazure.storageclient.cloudblobcontainer_members.aspx) acts on a single container.

Parameter	REST API	Client Library
List Containers	Using the GET operator, we can retrieve a list of containers for our storage account. The request URI is in the form http://<account>.blob.core.windows.net/?comp=list, where <account> will be replaced with our account name. The request will retrieve the entire list of containers (up to 5,000 items at a time). If a storage account has more than 5,000 containers, a continuation token will be returned, so the full list can be paginated by making subsequent requests and including this continuation token.	The CloudBlobClient.ListContainers method (http://msdn.microsoft.com/en-us/library/microsoft.windowsazure.storageclient.cloudblobclient.listcontainers.aspx) is used to list the containers in a storage account. The overloads ListContainers(<prefix>) is used to list only the containers whose names begin with the prefix, and ListContainers(<prefix>,<details>) is used to specify the level of detail to be returned. Detail options are passed as ContainerListingDetails, and the options are All, Metadata, and None.
Create Containers	Using the PUT operator, we can create a new container for our storage account. The request URI is in the form http://<account>.blob.core.windows.net/<container>?restype=container where <account> will be replaced with our account name and <container> is the name of the new container. If the container already exists, the operation will fail.	The CloudBlobContainer.Create or CloudBlobContainer.CreateIfNotExists methods are used to create a container in our storage account.

Parameter	REST API	Client Library
Get Container Properties	Using the GET/HEAD operator, we can retrieve all the user-defined metadata and system properties for a specified container. The request URI is in the form http://<account>.blob.core.windows.net/<container>?restype=container where <account> will be replaced with our account name and <container> is the name of the container. In addition to a container's metadata, there are a series of properties such as the Last-Modified date and ETag. Retrieving the properties of a container returns both the system properties and any metadata.	The CloudBlobContainer.FetchAttributes method is used to query the system properties and container metadata. The properties are then accessed via the CloudBlobContainer.Properties property.
Get Container Metadata	Using the GET/HEAD operator, we can retrieve only the user-defined metadata for a specified container. The request URI is in the form http://<account>.blob.core.windows.net/<container>?restype=container&comp=metadata where <account> will be replaced with our account name and <container> is the name of the container. Each container can have up to 8 KB of metadata associated with it. We can use this metadata for a variety of purposes such as categorizing the contents of the container (Christmas videos, photos of RVs, and so on). Getting the metadata returns only the metadata.	After calling the CloudBlobContainer.FetchAttributes method, metadata are accessed via the CloudBlobContainer.Metadata property.
Set Container Metadata	Using the PUT operator, we can set one or more of the user-defined metadata for a specified container. The request URI is in the form http://<account>.blob.core.windows.net/<container>?restype=container&comp=metadata where <account> will be replaced with our account name and <container> is the name of the container.	The CloudBlobContainer.SetMetadata method is used to add metadata to a container.

Parameter	REST API	Client Library
Get Container ACL	Using the GET/HEAD operator, we can get the access control list for a specified container. The request URI is in the form `http://<account>.blob.core.windows.net/<container>?restype=container&comp=acl` where `<account>` will be replaced with our account name and `<container>` is the name of the container. There are three levels of permissions that can be applied to a container: • Full public read, in which both container and blob data can be read by anonymous users • Public read access for blobs only, in which only blob data can be read by anonymous users • No public read access The permissions on a container are known as the Access Control List, or ACL, a term also applied to folder permissions on the Windows OS.	The `CloudBlobContainer.GetPermissions` is used to retrieve the container's ACL.
Set Container ACL	Using the PUT operator, we can set the access control list for a specified container. The request URI is in the form `http://<account>.blob.core.windows.net/<container>?restype=container&comp=acl` where `<account>` will be replaced with our account name and `<container>` is the name of the container.	The `CloudBlobContainer.SetPermissions` method is used to set a container's ACL.
Delete Container	Using the DELETE operator, we can mark the container to be deleted. The container is not deleted right away, but later during a garbage cleanup process. The request URI is in the form `http://<account>.blob.core.windows.net/<container>?restype=container` where `<account>` will be replaced with our account name and `<container>` is the name of the container.	The `CloudBlobContainer.Delete` method is used to delete a container.

Working with blobs

Working with blobs using the REST interface is as easy as working with containers. The same PUT/GET/DELETE/HEAD operators are used with slightly different request URIs. In the client library, the CloudBlob class (http://msdn.microsoft.com/en-us/library/ee773197.aspx) is used to interact with individual blobs. Another useful class for working with blobs is the BlobRequest class (http://msdn.microsoft.com/en-us/library/microsoft.windowsazure.storageclient.protocol.blobrequest.aspx). The BlobRequest class has many similar methods to the CloudBlob class, and also includes the methods for working with blocks in block blobs.

Parameter	REST API	Client Library
List Blobs	Using the GET operator, we can retrieve a list of blobs in a container. The request URI is in the form http://<account>.blob.core.windows.net/<container>?restype=container&comp=list, where <account> will be replaced with our account name and <container> is the name of the container we're retrieving the list from. The request will retrieve the entire list of blobs in <container> (up to 5,000 items at a time). If a container has more than 5,000 blobs, a continuation token will be returned. The full list can be paginated by including the continuation token in subsequent requests.	The CloudBlobContainer.ListBlobs method is used to return a list of all blobs in a container.
Create Blob	Using the PUT operator, we can create a new blob in a container. The request URI is in the form http://<account>.blob.core.windows.net/<container>/<blob> where <account> will be replaced with our account name, <container> is the name of the container, and <blob> is the name of the blob. Note that all blobs in a container must have a unique name for that container! Also, creating a blob doesn't actually "create" the blob; it just reserves space for the blob. The blob isn't created until its contents are uploaded to the blob.	A blob is not created until its contents are uploaded. For smaller files, the simplest method is to use the CloudBlob.UploadFile method. For large page or block blobs, the methods for creating a blob differ.
Get Blob	Using the GET operator, we can retrieve a blob, blob properties, and metadata in a container. The request URI is in the form http://<account>.blob.core.windows.net/<container>/<blob> where <account> will be replaced with our account name, <container> is the name of the container, and <blob> is the name of the blob.	To retrieve a specific blob, we use one of the download methods such as CloudBlob.DownloadToFile.

Parameter	REST API	Client Library
Get Blob Properties	Using the `HEAD` operator, we can retrieve a blob's properties and metadata in a container. The request URI is in the form `http://<account>.blob.core. windows.net/<container>/<blob>` where `<account>` will be replaced with our account name, `<container>` is the name of the container, and `<blob>` is the name of the blob. This will not retrieve the blob contents, only the properties and metadata.	For retrieving properties and metadata, we call `CloudBlob. FethAttributes`, and access the specific information we want via `CloudBlob.Properties` and `CloudBlob. Metadata`.
Set Blob Properties	Using the `PUT` operator, we can set a blob's properties in a container. The request URI is in the form `http://<account>.blob.core.windows.net/ <container>/<blob>?comp=properties` where `<account>` will be replaced with our account name, `<container>` is the name of the container, and `<blob>` is the name of the blob.	To set a blob's properties, we call `CloudBlob. SetProperties`.
Get Blob Metadata	Using the `GET/HEAD` operator, we can retrieve a blob's metadata in a container. The request URI is in the form `http://<account>.blob.core.windows. net/<container>/<blob>?comp=metadata` where `<account>` will be replaced with our account name, `<container>` is the name of the container, and `<blob>` is the name of the blob.	For retrieving properties and metadata, we call `CloudBlob. FethAttributes`, and access the specific information we want via `CloudBlob.Properties` and `CloudBlob. Metadata`.
Set Blob Metadata	Using the `PUT` operator, we can set a blob's metadata in a container. he request URI is in the form `http://<account>.blob.core.windows.net/ <container>/<blob>?comp=metadata` where `<account>` will be replaced with our account name, `<container>` is the name of the container, and `<blob>` is the name of the blob.	To add metadata to a blob, we call the `CloudBlob. SetMetadata` method.
Delete Blob	Using the `DELETE` operator, we can mark a blob to be deleted. The blob is not deleted right away, but later during a garbage cleanup process. The request URI is in the form `http://<account>.blob.core.windows. net/<container>/<blob>` where `<account>` will be replaced with our account name, `<container>` is the name of the container, and `<blob>` is the name of the blob.	In the client library, to delete a specific blob, we'd call `CloudBlob.Delete`

Parameter	REST API	Client Library
Lease Blob	The request URI is in the form `http://<account>.blob.core.windows.net/<container>/<blob>?comp=lease` where `<account>` will be replaced with our account name, `<container>` is the name of the container, and `<blob>` is the name of the blob. The action is passed in the request header in the `x-ms-lease-action` property. Note that a lease on a blob is a lock, to make sure only one process can make changes to the blob at any given time. Leases are for one minute, which can be renewed. We can acquire, renew, release, and break a lease using the API. The difference between releasing a lease and breaking it is that releasing a lease will make the blob available immediately, where breaking it will allow the blob to be modified once the lease expires.	There is currently no way to manage leases via the client library. Steve Marx, from the Azure Team, has an example of how to manage leases on his blog at `http://blog.smarx.com/posts/leasing-windows-azure-blobs-using-the-storage-client-library`.
Snapshot Blob	Using the `PUT` operator, we can create a read-only copy of a blob in a container, called a snapshot. The request URI is in the form `http://<account>.blob.core.windows.net/<container>/<blob>?comp=snapshot` where `<account>` will be replaced with our account name, `<container>` is the name of the container, and `<blob>` is the name of the blob. This method is useful as a form of version control, to provide history of edits, or as a recovery strategy where blobs are frequently edited.	In the client library, we create a snapshot using the `CloudBlob.CreateSnapshot` method.
Copy Blob	Using the `PUT` operator, we can copy a blob in a container to a different location in the storage account. The request URI is in the form `http://<account>.blob.core.windows.net/<container>/<blob>` where `<account>` will be replaced with our account name, `<container>` is the name of the container, and `<blob>` is the name of the blob.	To copy a blob in the client library, we call `CloudBlob.CopyFromBlob`.
Create Blocks	Using the `PUT` operator, we can create a new block to be committed as part of a blob. The request URI is in the form `http://<account>.blob.core.windows.net/<container>/<blob>?comp=block&blockid=id` where `<account>` will be replaced with our account name, `<container>` is the name of the container, and `<blob>` is the name of the blob. The blockid is a unique name for the block, and you would replace the `id` with the block name following the `blockid=` expression.	In the client library, we call `BlobRequest.PutBlock` to upload a block.

Parameter	REST API	Client Library
Create Block List	Using the PUT operator, we create a list of blocks that a blob consists of. The request URI is in the form `http://<account>.blob.core.windows.net/<container>/<blob>?comp=blocklist` where `<account>` will be replaced with our account name, `<container>` is the name of the container, and `<blob>` is the name of the blob.	To upload a block list using the client library, we use `BlobRequest.PutBlockList`.
Get Block List	Using the GET operator, we retrieve a list of blocks that a blob consists of. The request URI is in the form `http://<account>.blob.core.windows.net/<container>/<blob>?comp=blocklist` where `<account>` will be replaced with our account name, `<container>` is the name of the container, and `<blob>` is the name of the blob.	To get the block list, we call the `BlobRequest.GetBlockList` method.

Summary

Blob Storage is an amazing storage mechanism in Windows Azure. Between the scalability factors, authorization security settings, and the Blob Storage API for easy access, this truly is a long-term solution for anyone wishing to utilize Windows Azure for any application or service. In this chapter, we gained an overview of the two types of blobs, created a storage service for our project, and examined the API and client library used to interact with containers and blobs. As mentioned, we will begin to use Blob Storage and the Blob Storage API in Chapter 9 of this book when we build the front-end of our application for "Spee-D Delivery" with "Jupiter Motors" web role.

7
Azure Table Storage

Another storage option in Windows Azure is Table Storage. In this chapter, we'll examine Table Storage and the Table Services API in further detail. Table Storage is a persistent repository that can scale to humongous proportions (unlike SQL Azure, which is limited to gigabytes per database). It is accessible by both REST—the Windows Azure Management Library and client libraries for ADO.NET Data Services.

In this chapter, we'll:

- Compare Table Storage with relational database tables
- Discuss some pros and cons of Table Storage
- See how to access Table Storage via REST or a .NET client library.
- Consider error handling when working with Table Storage

Table Storage versus database tables

For developers used to working with a relational database, Table Storage may seem like a step backwards. After further examination, we may begin to see Table Storage as a very powerful and flexible technology. Table Storage is not a relational mechanism, but simple relations can be maintained in application code. For developers interested in an object-based database, Table Storage may be closer to what is desired.

Tables in databases and Table Storage both have table names. Tables in Table Storage are composed of entities, which are similar to rows in a database table. Each entity has:

- A PartitionKey that is used to group entities onto the same partition
- A RowKey that uniquely identifies a row within a partition
- A system-maintained Timestamp
- Properties that are similar to columns in a database table

Properties are stored and retrieved as `<name,value>` pairs. The PartitionKey has a very important use. As the Azure Fabric optimizes itself, tables will be moved from disk partition to partition, and even split across partitions. The PartitionKey is used to make sure all entities that belong together are kept together, thereby increasing the performance of the table. The PartitionKey and RowKey together make a primary key for the table. It's important to understand PartitionKeys, and we are going to cover them in further detail in the coming sections.

One of the biggest differences between Table Storage and a database table is the lack of a fixed schema in Table Storage, as seen in the next diagram. In a database table, there is a fixed schema with all rows having the same number of columns, and all values in the same column having the same data type. By contrast, all entities have a PartitionKey and a RowKey, but each can have a varying number of properties, and properties with the same name can have values of different types.

Because Table Storage is not relational, there are no foreign key constraints — all relations are "loose", and must be maintained by application logic. This adds some additional development, along with introducing a great deal of flexibility in the system.

At the most basic level, if a web application has drop-down lists for countries or states, Table Storage is a perfect mechanism for holding this information. Countries and states are small examples — Table Storage is optimized for thousands to millions of entries. And tables are queryable via LINQ and ADO.NET Data Services, giving them a database-like functionality. Another, larger example wouldbe to use Table Storage as a repository for auto-complete suggestions, such as the auto-complete in Google's search box.

A more complex use for Table Storage would be to serve as an object database. Each table would contain a number of different objects, identified by their partition keys. The RowKey would be used to identify property groups or sub-objects, and each entity would be a property of the object. Specific objects can be retrieved by their PartitionKey, specific property sets by the RowKey, and the object can be rehydrated by application code.

```
Contacts Table
PartitionKey    RowKey       Properties
BillGates       NameRow      FirstName,Bill:LastName,Gates
BillGates       CareerRow    Company,Microsoft|Gates Foundation
BillGates       PersonalRow  Hobby,Philanthropy
LarryEllison    NameRow      FirstName,Larry:LastName,Ellison
LarryEllison    CareerRow    Company,Oracle
LarryEllison    PersonalRow  Hobby,Sailing
SteveJobs       NameRow      FirstName,Steve:LastName,Jobs
SteveJobs       CareerRow    Company,Hewlett-Packard|Apple|NeXT|Pixar
SteveJobs       PersonalRow  Hobby,Disrupting Markets
```

In the example shown in the preceding screenshot, the `Company` property contains a pipe-delimited string as its value. Retrieving the individual values is not a standard operation—this string would need to be split on the client side before the individual properties can be accessed. But using this technique allows for a flexible data storage schema. While using a strategy like this gives us a great deal of flexibility, it can place a burden on application development and maintenance, as we would essentially be building our own **object-relational mapping (ORM)** engine.

Some of the good stuff

One of the biggest features of Table Storage may be its size. Table Storage is scalable, and tables can be massive, occupying terabytes of space and containing billions of entities. There are no set limits as to the number of tables or the size of each table. Naturally, all of this data will not exist on a single node. Tables will be spread out over numerous servers, and "hot partitions" will be load balanced and located for efficient delivery. Table Storage is persistent, so if we turn our Azure instance off, our data will be restored when we turn our instance back on.

There are a couple data access options for Table Storage too. We can access tables directly via a REST API, or we can query a table via a subset of LINQ and a client library for ADO.NET Data Services.

As with other forms of data access, table queries can timeout. Each table query is limited to 1,000 results or 5 seconds of execution, whichever comes first. However, instead of throwing an error when an execution maximum is reached, a partial resultset is returned with a continuation token. Passing the continuation token back in a subsequent request enables the query to start again from that point.

Updates and deletes are performed with optimistic concurrency. This means it's up to us to determine if we should preserve any changes made prior to our update, or to just overwrite these changes.

Limitations of Table Storage

There are some limitations to using Table Storage. To start with, each entity can have a maximum size of 1 MB. The PartitionKey and RowKey are limited to string data type, and have a maximum size of 1 KB each; however, when accessing entities via REST, there is a practical limit on the length of the PartitionKey and RowKey. This stems from a limitation in HTTP.SYS, the "listener" for web requests, and the HTTP/1.1 protocol, which limits URI length to 260 characters. This is not the entire URL, merely the parameter portion of the URL. Given the following example URL, the portion in bold cannot be longer than 260 characters:

```
http://<account>.table.core.windows.net/
<tablename>(PartitionKey="keyvalue",RowKey="keyvalue")
```

There are a maximum number of 255 properties per entity — 252 user-defined properties and three fixed properties (PartitionKey, RowKey, and Timestamp). Property names can be repeated from entity to entity, but a property name must be unique within an entity. The entity Timestamp is read only, and it is recommended not to build applications that access this property as its use may change in future versions of Azure Table Storage.

Because there are no keys to link tables together, the ADO.NET Data Services methods that deal with links are unavailable to use, including `AddLink`, `DetachLink`, and `SetLink`. All referential integrity must be handled in the application code.

There is also no way to retrieve a specific property directly from the table. Instead, we must retrieve the complete entity and parse what we want in our code. Likewise, we cannot update or delete a single property. Instead, a complete entity is retrieved and parsed, properties are changed or removed, and the complete entity is rewritten to the table.

Unlike a database, our table data cannot be sorted or grouped before being returned to us. In SQL Server, it would be trivial to return the top 10 customers based on total sales. In Table Storage, this is not possible natively. Our application would need to retrieve all the customers, calculate the total sales, and then sort the list.

Adding Table Storage to an Azure account

By default, there are no services added to Azure accounts — these must be created after the account has been set up. When a simple storage service is created (as we did in *Chapter 6, Azure Blob Storage*), it includes all three storage mechanisms.

After a storage service has been added, the endpoints for all three services are displayed together, as shown in the following screenshot:

```
Cloud Storage
  Endpoints:                                              To access storage:
  http://speeddelivery.blob.core.windows.net/            Download Windows
  http://speeddelivery.queue.core.windows.net/           Azure SDK
  http://speeddelivery.table.core.windows.net/
```

Accessing Table Storage

For security purposes, each request to Table Storage must be authenticated using the 256-bit shared keys created when we added the storage service. Table Storage can be directly accessed via REST, or queried using a subset of LINQ. The REST interface allows languages such as Java, PHP, and Ruby to consume Table Storage, while client libraries for ADO.NET Data Services are limited to the .NET languages.

Each request made via the REST API has a different set of required headers, and the body of each request is Atom format. Queries made via the REST API will return either 1,000 records, or run for 5 seconds (a total of 30 seconds from scheduling/processing to completion). If a query crosses these boundaries, a continuation token will be returned, which can be used in a subsequent request. Responses from the REST API are in AtomPubformat (`http://en.wikipedia.org/wiki/Atom_(standard)`). The ADO.NET Data Services client libraries do not have query boundaries.

An important API header property is `x-ms-version`. Just as .NET allows multiple versions of the same libraries to be coexist in the **Global Assembly Cache (GAC)**, multiple versions of the Table Storage API will also coexist. This is an optional property, but if this property is left blank, the default library will be the most basic library available. If we are targeting specific API features in our application, or want to ensure no part of our application will break when the API is updated, we need to include this property. The value is a date stamp, so the header property for the April 2009 API would read `x-ms-version: 2009-04-14`.

Third-party products are being developed that allow us to work directly with tables in a more friendly way than coding. Two such examples are TableXplorer found at `http://clumsyleaf.com/products/tablexplorer`, and MyAzureStorage found at `https://www.myazurestorage.com/`.

Working with tables

The client class for working with tables via .NET and the Azure Managed Library is `Microsoft.WindowsAzure.StorageClient.CloudTableClient`. The methods listed in the following table are methods of this class, unless specified otherwise. The documentation for this class can be found at `http://msdn.microsoft.com/en-us/library/microsoft.windowsazure.storageclient.cloudtableclient.aspx`.

Documentation for the REST library can be found at `http://msdn.microsoft.com/en-us/library/dd179423.aspx`. The `CloudTableClient` class is more user-friendly than the REST API, but the REST API can accomplish all the necessary tasks.

The base URI for accessing tables via the REST API is `http://<myaccount>.table.core.windows.net/Tables`. The different HTTP verbs (POST, GET, DELETE) are used to determine the action, and parameters (such as the table name) are specified in the request body.

Table names must follow a naming convention:

- Names can only be alphanumeric
- Length must be between 3 to 63 characters
- The name cannot begin with a number
- Names are case insensitive

Operation	REST API	Client Library
Creating tables	We use the POST method to the base URI (shown above) to create a new table. The table name is in `<TableName>` element of the request body.	The `CreateTable(<tablename>)` method creates a blank table, but will fail if the table already exists. `CreateTableIfNotExist(<tablename>)` will create a blank table only if it does not exist. If we want our tables to be based on a class in our application, we can use the `CreateTablesFromModel` method.
		If we want or need to create tables asynchronously, we can use the `BeginTableCreate` or `BeginCreateTableIfNotExists` method. Each of these have a corresponding `End` method as well.
Querying a list of tables	Using the GET method, we can retrieve a list of tables in our storage account. There is no request body for this operation.	The `ListTables` method returns a list of the tables in our storage account. If we want to check for the existence of a particular table, we can use the `DoesTableExist` method. For asynchronous methods, we can utilize the `BeginListTablesSegmented` method.

Operation	REST API	Client Library
Deleting a table	The DELETE method is used to delete a single table. The table name is specified in the URI such as http://<myaccount>. table.core.windows.net/ Tables('<mytable>').	Not surprisingly, the DeleteTable or DeleteTableIfExist method is used to delete a table. For asynchronmously deleting tables, we utilize the BeginDeleteTable and BeginDeleteTableIfExist methods.

A note about table deletion: The actual table deletion is not immediate. The table is merely marked for deletion and becomes immediately inaccessible and the actual deletion occurs during garbage collection at a later time. Depending on the size of the table, it can take at least 40 seconds to delete the table. If we try to access a table while it is being deleted, we'll receive a status code of 409 in the response, along with an error message alerting that the table is being deleted.

Working with entities

The base URI for working with entities via the REST API is http://<account>. table.core.windows.net/<tablename>. Note that the specific table name is specified as part of the URI, unlike when we were working with tables. Entity properties are specified in the request body, which is in Atom format. Response bodies are also in Atom format. Documentation for entity operations via REST API can be found at http://msdn.microsoft.com/en-us/library/dd179375.aspx.

When working through the .NET client library, we create a DataServiceContext and use LINQ queries to perform the desired operation. Documentation for the DataServiceContext can be found at http://msdn.microsoft.com/en-us/ library/system.data.services.client.dataservicecontext.aspx. At the time of writing, LINQ is only partially supported by design. Information on writing LINQ queries for table documentation can be found at http://msdn.microsoft.com/en-us/library/dd894039.aspx.

It's not possible to work directly with individual properties. Instead, we must retrieve the entity containing the property, manipulate the property, and then update the entity back in the cloud.

Operation	REST API	Client Library
Inserting entities	The POST method is used to insert a new entity into the table specified in the URI. Entity properties are sent as child elements of the <properties> element.	After we create a DataServiceContext to our table, we then use the AddObject method to add the entity, and the SaveChanges method to add the entity to the table.
Querying entities	Querying entities from a table uses the GET method. The REST API has a simple query syntax, with either the keys or a filter string passed in the URI. Because values are passed in the querystring, the following characters must be encoded before the filter string is assembled: /, ?, :, @, &, =, + , and $. There is no request body, as the entire request is contained in the URI. If the PaginationKey and RowKey are known, a specific entity can be retrieved using the following URI: http://<account>.table.core.windows.net/<table>(PartitionKey='<partitionkey>', RowKey='<rowkey>'). If we want to retrieve a filtered list of entities, we can use the following URI: http://<account>.table.core.windows.net/<table>()?$filter=<query-expression>. The $filter option is part of the Atom Publishing Protocol. More information on the $filter option can be found at http://www.odata.org/docs/[MC-APDSU].htm#_Toc246716529. Recall that queries made via the REST API have boundaries, and exceeding the boundaries will result in a partial recordset and a continuation token being returned. Documentation on pagination with continuation tokens can be found at http://msdn.microsoft.com/en-us/library/dd135718.aspx. The response body will include an opaque property called an ETag. The ETag is considered opaque because we cannot alter its value, nor should we use this value as an identifier in our code (as there is a date/time component, the ETag won't have a consistent value). The ETag is used by the back-end of the REST API for concurrency when making changes to entities.	When we query ADO.NET Data Services using LINQ via a client library, there are no query boundaries. The query will return the full recordset, and will process up to the configured global timeout values. For examples of LINQ queries, refer to the *Writing LINQ Queries* section at http://msdn.microsoft.com/en-us/library/dd894039.aspx.

Operation	REST API	Client Library

Updating entities: Azure uses optimistic concurrency, and assumes that updates will not affect each other, so resources are not locked. This is similar to optimistic concurrency in a database system.	We use the `PUT` method to a specific entity, as defined by the PartitionKey and RowKey combination. The URI looks just the same as when querying a specific entity:
	
	`http://<account>.`
	`table.core.windows.net/`
	`<table>(PartitionKey="<PartitionKey>",`
	`RowKey="<RowKey>")`
	
	The entity is contained in the request body. The ETag returned as part of the initial query must also be returned for concurrency. If the ETag returned matches the one on the entity, the update will be performed. If the ETag does not match, this indicates that the entity was changed since it was retrieved, and a **Precondition Failed** (response code 412) will be returned. Should this happen, we need to retrieve the latest version of the entity, perform the modifications again, and resubmit the update. An update can be forced by setting the `If-Match` request header parameter to the wildcard character "*".
		The `DataServiceContext` maintains the Etags for us, and handles the concurrency checking. After retrieving the entity or entities we want to modify, we make our changes and then update the data context using the `UpdateObject` method. The `SaveChanges` method then propagates the changes back to the table.

Merging Entities: The merge operation is used to combine the properties sent in the request with the properties of a specific entity. The merge method doesn't remove or change properties, it only adds them to an existing entity.	We use the `MERGE` method to combine two entities, as defined by the PartitionKey and RowKey combination. The URI looks just the same as when querying a specific entity:
	
	`http://<account>.`
	`table.core.windows.net/`
	`<table>(PartitionKey="<PartitionKey>",`
	`RowKey="<RowKey>")`
	
	The request body should contain the properties to be merged with the entity referenced in the URI. Concurrency is handled the same as with updates— an ETag is verified before an entity is merged, and if the ETags match, the merge is performed.
		As a merge is a form of an update, we use the same methods to merge as we do to update.

Operation	REST API	Client Library

Deleting entities: As with tables, entity is first marked for deletion and made inaccessible, then deleted via garbage collection at a later time.	We use the DELETE method to remove a specific entity, as defined by the PartitionKey and RowKey combination. The URI looks just the same as when querying a specific entity:
	
	`http://<account>.`
	`table.core.windows.net/`
	`<table>(PartitionKey="<PartitionKey>",`
	`RowKey="<RowKey>")`
	
	There is no request body, as the entity to be removed is identified specifically in the querystring. Concurrency is handled the same as with updates. An ETag is checked prior to deletion and, if the ETags match, the entity is marked for deletion.
		In our DataService Context, we call the DeleteObject method to remove the entity from the context, and then the SaveChanges method to propagate the change to the cloud.

We must follow naming rules for naming properties. Property names can contain alphanumeric characters and underscore, but cannot contain any extended or special characters. Property values can be one of eight types, with limitations on value ranges or size as described in the following table:

Value type	Description
Binary	A byte array, up to 64 KB in size. For large binary objects, consider using Blob Storage and making a pointer to the blob a property value.
Boolean	Boolean `true`/`false` value type.
DateTime	UTC time. As this is a 64-bit value, the valid range of dates is 1/1/1601 to 12/31/9999.
Double	A floating point value type. This is the only value type that can be used for decimal numbers. This is a 64-bit type.
GUID	A standard 128-bit globally unique identifier.
Int	A 32-bit signed integer. It has values ranging from -2,147,483,648 to 2,147,483,647.
Int64	A 64-bit signed integer. It has values ranging from -9,223,372,036,854,775,808 to 9,223,372,036,854,775,807.
String	Encoded UTF-16. Strings can be of a maximum size of 64 KB.

If we are using LINQ to query Table Storage, the property values will be inferred when the data are returned. However, if we are utilizing the REST API, property values will be returned as string data, which we will need to convert to the proper type in our application.

Entity Group Transactions

The examples we have seen in earlier sections focus on operations against a single entity. But what if we want to update all entities having the same partition key? Using the client library, we can perform multiple entity transaction. In our data context, we can queue a number of create/update/delete commands before committing the changes with the SaveChanges method. There are a few rules and limitations regarding Entity Group Transactions:

- Each command group can contain up to 100 commands.
- Operations can be performed only on entities with the same partition key.
- As the name implies, the commands are executed as an all-or-nothing transaction. If one command fails, the entire set is rolled back.
- The entire group can be only 4 MB in size. This means insertions of a large number of entities may need to be split into several groups.
- An entity can appear only once. We cannot insert an entity at the beginning of the group and then update it later.
- Commands are executed in the order they were inserted into the group.
- Concurrency is checked on the server. If an entity's ETags do not match, no change will be made and the entire command group fails.

Entity Group Transactions can be performed with either the REST API or the .NET Client Library. Microsoft's guidance on Entity Group Transactions can be found at http://msdn.microsoft.com/en-us/library/dd894038.aspx.

Choosing a PartitionKey

In order to store the massive amount of data and quickly return queries against this data, tables may be partitioned across thousands of nodes. This is where the partition key fits into the storage scheme—all entities with the same partition key will be kept together. Different entities from the same table may be served from different nodes, but every entity with the same partition key will be served from the same node. In our Contacts example we have seen earlier, all the BillGates records will be kept together, and all of the SteveJobs records would be kept together, which may be a different node than the BillGates records.

The Azure Fabric constantly monitors traffic to our partitions, and replicates active partitions to multiple nodes in order to satisfy traffic demands. Selecting a partition key becomes an important balance between query performance and response time. The smaller our partitions, the more nodes our table can be spread over. However, if we split apart entities that are frequently returned in the same resultset, we can degrade query performance.

Microsoft offers some advice on choosing a good PartitionKey:

- Identify the properties that will most commonly be used in filters. This is our list of important properties.

- Narrow the list of important properties down to a couple of the most important properties. These are our key candidates.

- Rank the key candidates in order of importance. If there is only one key property, that's our PartitionKey. If there are two, they should become our PartitionKey and RowKey. If there are more than two, the key properties can be concatenated into single keys with composite values.

- If the PartitionKey cannot be guaranteed to be unique, add a unique identifier to the key.

- Finally, a reality check—is the chosen PartitionKey likely to result in entities that are too large or too small?

Final confirmation of a good key choice will come by choosing a sample dataset, performing stress tests on our table, and then tweaking the PartitionKey if necessary.

Exception handling

Designing a robust application means handling the exceptions and errors that may arise at regular intervals. The following sections cover some of the more common categories of exceptions that may be encountered. How these exceptions are dealt with depends on the design and purpose of the application. Exception handling is entirely in the hands of the application developer.

Retry on exceptions

If the data matters, our application should retry the operation when the response code indicates something other than success. For applications with an end user, it may be sufficient to guide the user through a series of steps to retry the operation. For unattended applications, local retry queues, event logs/notifications, and increasing times between attempts may need to be implemented.

Network issues and connections being closed can result in an operation failing to reach the server. And although these should be rare, timeout exceptions can occur while an entity is being updated or propagated. The time interval between attempts should be increased if these errors occur multiple times.

Not every exception should have a retry. If we're attempting to delete an entity, and we receive a response that the entity does not exist, there is no need to reattempt the deletion.

Exceptions on retry

It's very possible that a server-side operation may succeed, but a network or timeout error prevents proper notification of success. A retry will then result in an error message that indicates the first operation was successful. For instance, if we successfully insert an entity, and a network timeout results in our application retrying the operation, we'll receive an **entity already exists** error. It would not be a good idea to retry the insertion in this circumstance because we'll be in a never-ending loop. One way to handle this situation gracefully is to query the table before an insert is attempted, to make sure the entity does not already exist.

Concurrency conflicts

In update and delete operations, an ETag mismatch will result in a **Precondition Failed** response. In this situation, we need to either retrieve the updated entity, make our modification, and then attempt the update again, or cancel our update altogether.

Table errors and HTTP response codes

When using the REST API, exception information is contained in two places. Each table error is mapped to an HTTP status code in the header of the response. The HTTP status codes are standard codes, and are not as informative as the table error code in the response body. The header codes are useful for determining the result of an operation, but the <ExceptionDetails> in the response body should be manifested to the user, or written to the application logs.

The client library receives the more detailed message as part of the thrown exception.

Summary

In this chapter, we discussed some of the benefits and limitations of Table Storage. We discussed ways to manipulate tables and entities with both the REST API and the ADO.NET Data Services client library. With its massive scalability and powerful access options, Table Storage can be a very useful part of an Azure application.

8
Queue Storage

Besides Blob Storage and Table Storage, Queue Storage is the third type of simple storage option in Windows Azure. Queues are designed to be a reliable method for front-end servers to asynchronously communicate with back-end servers. Persistent queues provide a robust messaging system between the different tiers of our application, and decoupling front-and back-end servers from one another allows one end to scale independently of the other. As with Table and Blob Storage, there is both a rich client library and REST API, which can be leveraged to access Queue Storage.

In this chapter, we'll:

- Learn what Azure Queue Storage is
- Discuss why we would want to use a queue
- See how to access Queue Storage via REST or a .NET client library.

The ins and outs of queues

Looking at the following diagram, we can see where Queue Storage fits in with the rest of Windows Azure:

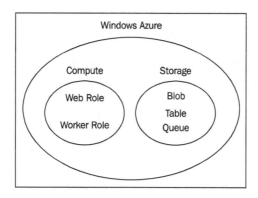

As one of the three simple storage options, Queue Storage is created when a storage service is added to an account. The Queue Storage endpoint is listed with the others when we view a storage service, as shown here:

A single Azure account can have any number of queues. Each queue is composed of messages, each of which carries the data or processing instructions that need to be acted upon by the back-end servers (refer to the next diagram).

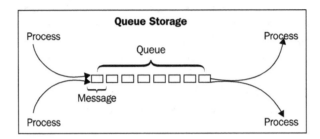

There is no enforced limit to the number of messages in a queue, although there is a practical limit to the number of messages we'd want stacked up at any given time. Messages with a long latency in the queue are an indication that either the back-end processes need to be further optimized, or we need to scale out some additional back-end servers.

Each message is simply an XML document, in Atom format; messages are limited to 8 KB in size. If the data to be processed are greater than 8 KB, the data should be stored in a blob or table, and processing instructions sent in the message. In addition to the messages, each queue can have up to 8 KB of metadata associated with it. Metadata are stored as name-value pairs.

The idea behind a queue is to provide a way for different processes to communicate with one another in an asynchronous manner. A queue is best used when there is not tight time dependence between the completion of one action and when the subsequent one completes. A queue should be used when the message must get processed, but no one is waiting for the processing to happen. However, queues can be used in many different scenarios, allowing flexibility in application tiers to perform a structured workflow asynchronously.

Reasons to use a queue

If we have to justify to a project manager why we should implement queues, here are a few points we can use:

- When any application crashes, any in-process session information is lost. However, in the case of Queue Storage, it is persistent and has recovery mechanisms if a message fails to process.

- Queues allow processes to scale independently. One common arrangement is for a front-end process to call a back-end process, wait for the back end to complete, and then the front-end process performs its next action. There is a 1:1 relationship between front-end and back-end processes. By using a queue to pass processing instructions, processes can scale independently of one another; there can be 1:10 or 10:1 front-end to back-end process ratio. This independent scalability allows our application to absorb traffic surges in a better way.

- Using multiple queues allows work to be segregated by importance. Queues containing more important work can have more processes directed against them, or can have special services written for them.

- By decoupling application layers, the different processes can be written in different languages, and may exist in completely different locations.

Invisibility time and failover

In the points we discussed in the previous section, we mentioned a recovery mechanism if a message fails to process. Here's how that works:

- A GET request via the REST API or a query in the client library is prepared in our application. The request or query should specify a parameter called `visibilitytimeout`. The `visibilitytimeout` sets the amount of time (in seconds) that the message will be invisible to subsequent processes.

- A message is "dequeued", that is, it is read from the queue and marked as invisible to any further requests. The message technically stays in the queue, but is inaccessible.

- If the message processing succeeds, the message is marked for deletion and cleaned up later with garbage collection. It's important to delete the message before the `visibilitytimeout` expires, or we risk another process dequeuing and processing the message.

- If the message processing fails, the message becomes visible again after the `visibilitytimeout` has expired. As message processing is FIFO (First In, First Out), the next process reading from the queue will retrieve this message again, and the process starts over.

The process is outlined in the following diagram:

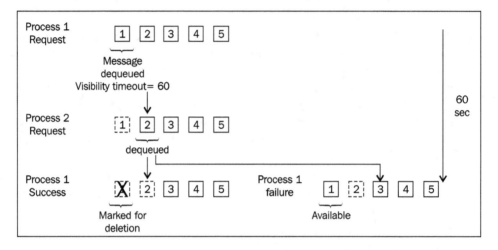

Choosing the right value for the `visibilitytimeout` parameter is important. If the invisibility time set is too short, the message may become available again while it is still being processed. On the other hand, if the processing time is too long, there will be added latency should the message processing fail. Considering the consequences, it's probably better to set the timeout a little longer.

Special handling for binary data

Binary data can be transmitted in XML, so that queued messages can contain binary data. The data will be processed as binary data. However, when the messages are dequeued, the data are Base-64 encoded, including the binary data. Our application would need to decode the binary data properly before processing the binary data.

Working with queues

The client class for working with queues via .NET code is `Microsoft.WindowsAzure.StorageClient.CloudQueue`. The methods listed here are methods of this class, unless specified otherwise. The documentation for this library can be found at `http://msdn.microsoft.com/en-us/library/microsoft.windowsazure.storageclient.cloudqueue.aspx`.

Documentation for the REST library for Queue Storage can be found at
`http://msdn.microsoft.com/en-us/library/dd179363.aspx`. The base URI for
accessing queues via the REST API is `http://<account>.queue.core.windows.net`.
To perform an operation on a specific queue, the URI is `http://<account>.queue.`
`core.windows.net/<queue>` and the different HTTP verbs (`PUT`, `GET`, `DELETE`) are
used to determine the action.

When using the REST API, every operation has an optional `timeout` parameter that
sets the processing timeout of the operation. If the operation does not complete by
the timeout, it will fail. The default value is 30 seconds, which is also the maximum
value that can be set.

As with Table and Blob Storage, the optional `x-ms-version` header should also be
used with Queue Storage requests.

Listing queues

Obtaining a list of queues is technically an action performed against the account,
rather than the collection of queues. As such, the base URI or client library class are
different than for the rest of the operations.

REST API

To list the queues in our account, a `GET` request is made to this URI:
`http://<account>.queue.core.windows.net?comp=list`. This will return
a list of up to 5,000 queues in our account. To shape the response, we can use
some optional URI parameters to filter the list:

Parameter	Description
`prefix`	Returns only such queues whose names begin with the specified prefix.
`marker`	Similar in function to the continuation tokens used for Table Storage. The `marker` parameter specifies where the query results begin. The results include a `NextMarker` parameter in the response body that can be used as the marker value for a subsequent query.
`maxresults`	Limits the query only to the specified number of results.
`include=metadata`	If this parameter is included, the queue's metadata will be included as part of the response.

Client library

The `CloudQueueClient` class is used to perform queue-related actions against the storage account. Documentation for this class can be found at `http://msdn.microsoft.com/en-us/library/microsoft.windowsazure.storageclient.cloudqueueclient.aspx`.

To obtain a list of queues, we use the `ListQueues` method, which has three overloads, as described in the following table:

Method signature	Description
`ListQueues()`	Returns all queues in our account.
`ListQueues(<prefix>)`	Returns all queues whose names begin with the specified prefix.
`CloudQueueClient.ListQueues (<prefix>, <QueueListingDetails>)`	Returns all queues whose names begin with the specified prefix, and includes the specified level of details. `QueueListingDetails` is an enum with three values specifying the level of detail—`All` (return all available details for each queue), `Metadata` (include metadata only), and `None` (return no details).

Creating queues

Because queues are addressable via URI, their names must be valid DNS names. There are four basic rules regarding queue names:

- The queue name can contain only letters, numbers, and "-"
- The queue name must begin and end with a letter only
- Queue names must be lowercase
- A queue name must be at least three characters, but shouldn't be longer than 63 characters

Metadata names must be valid C# identifiers. Metadata names are case insensitive when created or queried, but the case is preserved when the results are returned.

REST API

A `PUT` request is made to the base URI, naming the queue to be created. Queue metadata is passed in the headers, using `x-ms-meta-<name>:<value>`. Metadata names must follow the same naming rules as C# identifiers.

If the named queue exists, the queue service checks the metadata to see if the two queues are identical. If the metadata match, a 204 "No Content" response code is received. If the metadata do not match, a 409 "Conflict" is returned.

Client library

To create a queue in a client library, we create an instance of the CloudQueue class, with the name we want the queue to be set to the name of this instance. We then call the Create method to create the queue. Metadata are added as properties of the CloudQueue instance.

Deleting queues

A queue is not immediately deleted when the Delete method succeeds. Instead, the queue is marked as unavailable and is cleaned up at a later time via garbage collection.

REST API

The Delete method is used to delete the queue specified in the URI.

Client library

To delete a queue via the client library, we create an instance of the CloudQueue class pointing to the queue we want to delete, and call the Delete method.

Setting metadata

As users, we can define metadata that describe the queue. Note that metadata are added to the queue, not the messages. We can use queue metadata to easily identify the characteristics of a queue, such as adding messages or working on messages, or the types of messages that pass through the queue.

REST API

To add/delete metadata via the REST API, a PUT request is made against the URI http://<account>.queue.core.windows.net/<queue>?comp=metadata. Metadata are specified in the request header as x-ms-meta-<name>:<value>. If no metadata are specified in the header, all metadata are deleted from the queue.

Client library

To start, we create an instance of CloudQueue class, referencing a specific queue. Then we create a NameValueCollection containing the metadata. We then add this to the Metadata property of our instance, and call the SetMetadata method.

Getting metadata

The whole point of setting metadata is to be able to retrieve the metadata for later usage. Let's now see how to retrieve the metadata.

REST API

To retrieve the metadata, we use a GET request to the URI http://<account>. queue.core.windows.net/<queue>?comp=metadata. Metadata are returned as x-ms-meta-<name>:<value> headers. To assist in processing the headers, the x-ms-approximate-message-count:<count> header is also returned.

Client library

When we create an instance of the CloudClient pointing to a specific queue, the metadata are accessible as the Metadata property of the queue.

Working with messages

As message manipulations are actually actions performed against a queue, the message methods are also part of the CloudQueue class.

Documentation for the REST library can be found at http://msdn.microsoft.com/ en-us/library/dd135717.aspx. The base URI for accessing queues via the REST API is http://<account>.queue.core.windows.net/<queue>/messages.

To address a specific message by its ID, the URI is http://<account>.queue. core.windows.net/<queue>/messages/messageid?popreceipt=<messageid>. The different HTTP verbs (POST, GET, DELETE) are used to determine the action. Note that the specific queue name is specified as part of the URI. Message properties are specified in the request body, which is in Atom format. Response bodies are also in Atom format.

Parameter	Rest API	Client library
Put messages	A message is added to the end of a queue by submitting a `POST` request to `http://<account>.queue.core.windows.net/<queue>/messages`. The message is XML and is posted in the request body. Messages are limited to 8 KB in length, and must be able to be UTF-8 encoded. The optional `messagettl` querystring property can be used to set the time to live (in seconds) for the message. The default TTL is seven days, which is the maximum value. Should a message reside in a queue for more than the TTL, the message will be deleted.	A message is created as an instance of a `CloudQueueMessage`, and is added to a queue by calling the `AddMessage` method. There are two overloads— `AddMessage(<message>)` and `AddMessage(<message>,<time-to-live>)`.
Get messages	The `GET` method dequeues messages from the specified queue for processing. Messages are returned in the response body in XML format; the format is the same as what was specified under the Put Message request. There are two optional querystring parameters that can be utilized: • `numofmessages`: Sets the number of messages to be returned. The value can be from 1 (default) to 32. • `visibilitytimeout`: Sets the time in seconds the retrieved messages will be invisible. The maximum value can be of up to two hours. Default is 30 seconds. When messages are dequeued via a `GET` method, they are made invisible to other processes. Included in the response properties is a `PopReceipt`, which is a message identifier that must be passed back in the `DELETE` request.	To dequeue the next message in the queue, the `GetMessage()` method can be used. There are two overloads—`GetMessage()`, and `GetMessage(<visibilitytimeout>)`. To dequeue a number of messages, the `GetMessages(<numofmessages>)` or `GetMessages(<numofmessages>,<visibilitytimeout>)` are used.

Parameter	Rest API	Client library
Peek messages	Peeking works the same as getting messages, with one required parameter in the querystring. To peek at messages, we use a GET method to the URI http://<account>.queue.core.windows.net/<queue>/messages?peekonly=true. The only optional querystring parameter is numofmessages. Peeking at messages is similar to getting messages, but when we peek, a message is not marked as invisible. This allows us to examine the contents of a queue (such as how long messages have been hanging around), without affecting queue processing.	As with GET, there are two methods we can call: PeekMessage() peeks at the next message in the queue, while PeekMessages(<numofmessages>) is used to peek at multiple messages.
Delete messages	To delete a message, we use a DELETE request to the URI http://<account>.queue.core.windows.net/<queue>/messages/messageid?popreceipt=<string-value>. If we want to delete all messages in a queue, we make a DELETE request to http://<account>.queue.core.windows.net/<queue>/messages. If there are a lot of messages, the command may timeout before it completes. The DELETE method is not transactional, so in this case, the DELETE request can be reissued several times until all messages have been deleted. It is important for applications working with messages to delete them if processing is successful. Otherwise, once the visibility timeout expires, the messages will be available for processing again. When a delete operation is successful, messages are not immediately deleted. Messages are marked for deletion, which makes them unavailable to any process, and are cleaned up later by garbage collection.	In the client library, we use the DeleteMessage method. There are two overloads— DeleteMessage(<message>) or DeleteMessage(<messageid>,<popreceipt>). All messages are cleared from a queue by calling the Clear() method.

Summary

In this chapter, we looked at where queues fit into Windows Azure, how they operate, and how to interact with queues using the REST API and a client library. Queues can be used for a large variety of asynchronous operations, passing messages between tiers of our applications. Whether we're using messages to pass information, control workflows, or a combination of the two, we can tailor our queue to bring out the best in any application with many processes across our application in the cloud.

9
Web Role

Azure applications are separated into two functional groups—web roles and worker roles. To understand in simpler words, web roles are similar to websites, whereas worker roles are similar to background services. An account must include at least one instance of either a worker role or a web role, however, there is no restriction on the maximum number of allowable instances. In this chapter, we'll cover the following:

- An introduction to web roles
- Comparing web roles to traditional ASP.NET development
- Creating a sample web role
- Building the ASP.NET portal website for Jupiter Motors, as a web role

The role of the web

In Azure, a web role is an HTTP or HTTPS endpoint, and so a web role can include both front-end websites as well as web services. Web roles can also make outbound connections to web services via HTTP.

Web roles can access Azure storage services (queue, blob, or table) via either the REST API or Windows Azure Storage Client Library, and can also connect to SQL Azure. Azure uses IIS7 and supports FastCGI for interpreted languages such as PHP or native code. Azure supports additional IIS modules such as the URL rewrite module.

Web roles can be an important way to collect or distribute information. Information can be supplied or collected via web services, or users can access websites to perform any number of functions.

With a few small differences, web development using Azure is nearly identical to standard web development. Microsoft is making a concerted effort to support a number of platforms and languages. In our example, we'll use Visual Studio 2008 and VB.NET, but SDKs have been developed for PHP/Eclipse and Ruby.

At this point, our example web role is simply a web form to upload a picture of the production progress on our RV. In this chapter, we're going to develop the web form. We'll be using the local development fabric and a local SQL Server, and we'll discuss SQL Azure connections when we deploy our application.

Web roles, déjà vu, and ASP.NET

If you've ever travelled to a new place but felt like you've been there before, then you'll be prepared for Azure development. Most components between the web role and the ASP.NET web application are the same— .aspx pages, classes, web.config, among other things. New components to our web role include three new assembly references, a WebRole.vb (or WebRole.cs) file, and a trace listener addition in the Web.config file.

The new assembly references are:

- Microsoft.WindowsAzure.Diagnostics, which contains the diagnostics and logging classes
- Microsoft.WindowsAzure.ServiceRuntime, which allows the recycling of roles and also allows access to configuration settings
- Microsoft.WindowsAzure.StorageClient, which is the library for the Blob, Table, and Queue Storage REST interfaces

These three assemblies are referenced in addition to the other references we need in our application.

The new WebRole.vb (or WebRole.cs) file is just some template code for setting up the logging and diagnostics (VB code shown in further section).

Creating the solution and web role project

Now that we've discussed how similar Azure and ASP.NET development are, we need to start with something slightly different. In order to develop using Azure, we need to have the SDK and Visual Studio tools installed (refer to Chapter 3). These tools add new project and item templates that we need to use in Visual Studio.

To create our Azure project, open Visual Studio, start a new project, open the language (in our case, Visual Basic) and select **Cloud**. Under **Templates**, choose a **Windows Azure Cloud Service** and give a suitable name to the project.

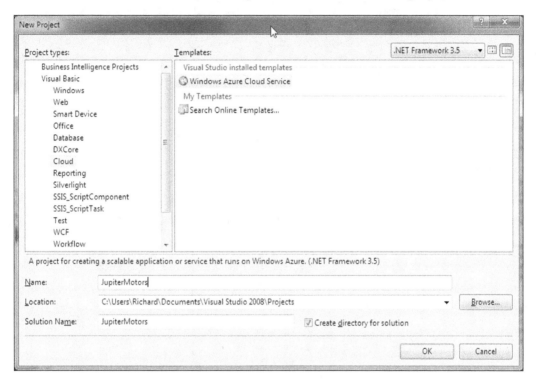

Once the solution and project is created by Visual Studio, we are prompted to add roles to our project. At this time, we only need to add a single web role to our project.

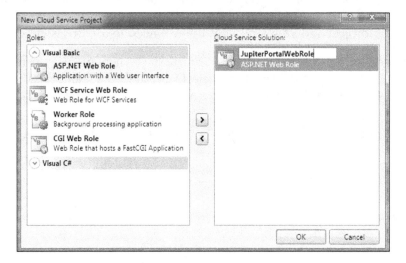

Our new project now looks like this:

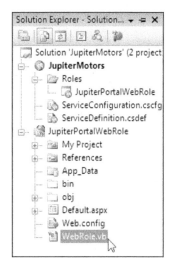

One of the new project components needed for Azure development is `WebRole.vb`. This file is automatically created when our web role was created, and contains the following boilerplate code:

```
Imports Microsoft.WindowsAzure.Diagnostics
Imports Microsoft.WindowsAzure.ServiceRuntime
```

```
Public Class WebRole
    Inherits RoleEntryPoint

    Public Overrides Function OnStart() As Boolean

        DiagnosticMonitor.Start("DiagnosticsConnectionString")

        ' For information on handling configuration changes
        ' see the MSDN topic at
          http://go.microsoft.com/fwlink/?LinkId=166357.
        AddHandler RoleEnvironment.Changing, AddressOf
                              RoleEnvironmentChanging

        Return MyBase.OnStart()

    End Function

    Private Sub RoleEnvironmentChanging(ByVal
                          sender As Object, ByVal e As
                          RoleEnvironmentChangingEventArgs)

        ' If a configuration setting is changing
        If (e.Changes.Any(Function(change)
        TypeOf change Is RoleEnvironmentConfigurationSettingChange))
        Then' Set e.Cancel to true to restart this role instance
            e.Cancel = True
        End If

    End Sub

End Class
```

Application diagnostics and logging in the cloud

Think of how we currently log our events and diagnostics. We have IIS logs and application logs to help us see things in the event of something not working. These logs live on our physical servers, and we can access them anytime we need. Now, think of how our application lives in Windows Azure. We don't have any physical machines to save logs or any control of IIS. How are we going to store our logs for debugging problems?

Fortunately, even Microsoft had to confront this problem and it came up with an appropriate answer. First, we need to ensure our application has a trace listener enabled; a **trace listener** is a link between our application and Azure's diagnostic tools. We need to confirm the following code is present in the `web.config` file:

```
<system.diagnostics>
    <trace>
        <listeners>
            <add type="Microsoft.WindowsAzure.Diagnostics.
DiagnosticMonitorTraceListener, Microsoft.WindowsAzure.Diagnostics,
Version=1.0.0.0, Culture=neutral, PublicKeyToken=31bf3856ad364e35"
                name="AzureDiagnostics">
                <filter type="" />
            </add>
        </listeners>
    </trace>
</system.diagnostics>
```

We don't have access to logs on physical servers, but then what do we have? When developing locally in our development fabric, we can see everything in the Development Fabric UI. To achieve this, run the application in debug mode and we will see that our development fabric starts (in Windows 7, we may need to enable the permission to "run as administrator" for the development fabric to start). Right-click on the fabric icon in the notifications area of your taskbar, and select the **Show Development Fabric UI** option as shown in the next screenshot:

This will open up the Development Fabric UI. From here, we can drill down into our web role instance to see everything we have set to log.

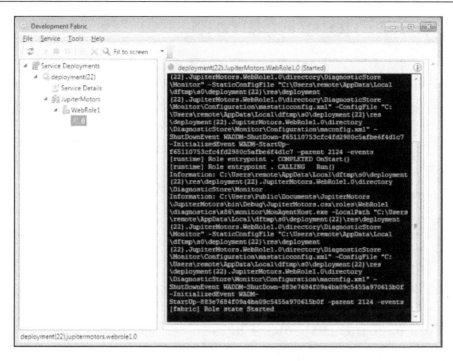

This is great news for local development, but what about logging in the cloud? Because we don't have our physical machines to store our logs on, and we don't have a Production Fabric UI, then what do we have? Well, the answer is we have Windows Azure Storage at our fingertips. Not only did Microsoft give us a way to keep this information in Windows Azure Storage, but they also built a nice way to log information in our code.

Specific information needs to be kept in a particular type of storage, whether it is Blob or Table Storage. The following is the correct storage type for each log:

- **Blob Storage**: IIS7 logs, Failed Request logs, Crash Dumps, and Custom Error logs
- **Table Storage**: Windows Azure logs, Windows Diagnostic infrastructure logs, Windows Event logs, and Performance Counters

At this point, our application doesn't include any logging. We're still developing locally, so we have the UI to debug. Before an application is released into the production cloud, it would be wise to add some type of logging and diagnostics. We will dig into this deeper in *Chapter 15, Deploying to Windows Azure.*

Jupiter Motors web role

Our web role for Jupiter Motors is a simple application structure. We have:

- `Default.aspx` page to use for navigating to other pages
- `UploadOrderPicture.aspx` page for our web form to upload pictures for an order
- `ViewOrders.aspx` page to see an order status and any uploaded pictures
- `Web.config` file and the new `WebRole.vb` file

Here is how our Portal pages will look like:

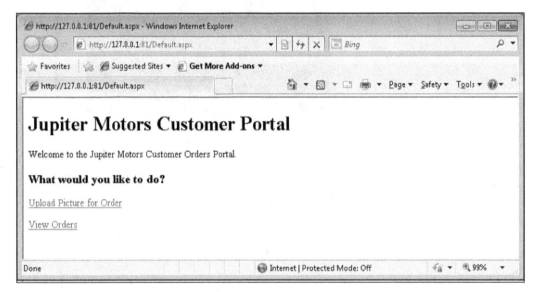

The following is what we see when we run the `UploadOrderPicture.aspx` page. Our web form will be used to select an order in production, select a photo to show the customer as an update, and upload this photo into Blob Storage. Once the picture is saved in Blob Storage, a record will be written to the `OrderPictures` table in our Portal database (that will eventually live in the SQL Azure cloud). This page will mainly be used by the production line to provide the photos of the RV being built.

The following screenshot shows the `ViewOrders.aspx` page. This page will be used mainly by customers to check the status of their orders and see photos of the RV in production.

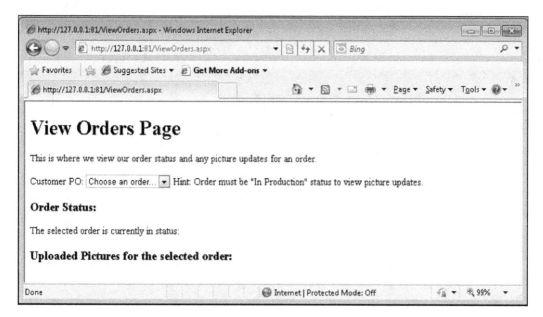

How do we get there? Here's our code!

In the following sections, we will see how similar programming for Azure is to programming for traditional ASP.NET websites; except for the Azure-specific code to collect diagnostic information and use Blob Storage, everything else is the same.

Additional stored procedures used by the web role

We'll use stored procedures so that we can encapsulate search and filtering logic in the database layer, which is most optimized for that type of processing. These stored procedures need to be created in the Portal database, and will retrieve data needed by the pages in the web role.

```
SET ANSI_NULLS ON
GO
SET QUOTED_IDENTIFIER ON
GO
CREATE PROCEDURE [dbo].[NewOrderPicture]
    -- Add the parameters for the stored procedure here
    @OrderHeaderID int,
    @PictureFile varchar(100)
AS
BEGIN

    SET NOCOUNT ON;

    Insert Into OrderPictures(OrderHeaderID, PictureFile, PictureDate)
    Values(@OrderHeaderID, @PictureFile, getdate())

END
GO

SET ANSI_NULLS ON
GO
SET QUOTED_IDENTIFIER ON
GO
CREATE PROCEDURE [dbo].[GetOrderStatusForOrderHeaderID]
@OrderHeaderID int
AS
BEGIN

    SET NOCOUNT ON;

    Select os.Description
```

```
    From OrderHeaders oh
    Join OrderStatuses os
           On oh.OrderStatusID = os.OrderStatusID
    Where oh.OrderHeaderID = @OrderHeaderID
END
GO


SET ANSI_NULLS ON
GO
SET QUOTED_IDENTIFIER ON
GO
CREATE PROCEDURE [dbo].[GetOrdersInProduction]

AS
BEGIN
    SET NOCOUNT ON;


    Select OrderHeaderID, CustomerPO From OrderHeaders
    Where OrderStatusID = 4
END
GO


SET ANSI_NULLS ON
GO
SET QUOTED_IDENTIFIER ON
GO


CREATE PROCEDURE [dbo].[GetOrders]

AS
BEGIN
    SET NOCOUNT ON;


    Select OrderHeaderID, CustomerPO From OrderHeaders
END
```

The following is the code for the `Default.aspx` HTML page:

```
<%@ Page Language="vb" AutoEventWireup="false" CodeBehind="Default.
aspx.vb" Inherits="WebRole1._Default" %>

<!DOCTYPE html PUBLIC "-//W3C//DTD XHTML 1.0 Transitional//EN"
"http://www.w3.org/TR/xhtml1/DTD/xhtml1-transitional.dtd">
<html xmlns="http://www.w3.org/1999/xhtml">
<head runat="server">
```

```
    <title></title>
</head>
<body>
    <form id="form1" runat="server">
    <div>
        <h1>
            Jupiter Motors Customer Portal
        </h1>
        <p>
            Welcome to the Jupiter Motors Customer Orders Portal.
        </p>
    </div>
    <div>
        <h3>
            What would you like to do?</h3>
        <p>
            <asp:LinkButton ID="lnkBntUploadPicture"
            runat="server">Upload Picture for Order</asp:LinkButton>
        </p>
        <p>
            <asp:LinkButton ID="lnkBtnViewOrders"
             runat="server">View Orders</asp:LinkButton>
        </p>
    </div>
    </form>
</body>
</html>
```

The following is the `Default.aspx` code-behind:

```
Partial Public Class _Default
    Inherits System.Web.UI.Page


    ''' <summary>
    ''' Redirects user to UploadOrderPicture.aspx
        when link button is clicked
    ''' </summary>
    ''' <param name="sender"></param>
    ''' <param name="e"></param>
    ''' <remarks></remarks>
    Protected Sub lnkBntUploadPicture_Click
                (ByVal sender As Object, ByVal e As EventArgs)
                Handles lnkBntUploadPicture.Click
        Response.Redirect("~/UploadOrderPicture.aspx")
    End Sub
```

```
'''    <summary>
'''    Redirects user to ViewOrders.aspx when link button is clicked
'''    </summary>
'''    <param name="sender"></param>
'''    <param name="e"></param>
'''    <remarks></remarks>
Protected Sub lnkBtnViewOrders_Click
              (ByVal sender As Object, ByVal e As EventArgs)
              Handles lnkBtnViewOrders.Click
    Response.Redirect("~/ViewOrders.aspx")
End Sub
End Class
```

The following is the `UploadOrderPictures.aspx` HTML file code:

```
<%@ Page Language="vb" AutoEventWireup="false" CodeBehind="UploadOrder
Picture.aspx.vb"
    Inherits="WebRole1.UploadOrderPicture" %>

<!DOCTYPE html PUBLIC "-//W3C//DTD XHTML 1.0 Transitional//EN"
"http://www.w3.org/TR/xhtml1/DTD/xhtml1-transitional.dtd">
<html xmlns="http://www.w3.org/1999/xhtml">
<head runat="server">
    <title></title>
</head>
<body>
    <form id="form1" runat="server">
    <div id="UploadPicture">
        <div>
            <h1>
                Welcome to the Upload Order Picture Page
            </h1>
            <p>
                This is where we will upload a picture or update the
                status of an order.
            </p>
        </div>
        <div>
            <h3>
                Upload a picture:
            </h3>
            <p>
                Order Number:
                <asp:DropDownList ID="ddlOrdersInProduction"
                                      runat="server" />
```

```
                    Hint: Order must be "In Production" status to upload
                                    picture for order.
            </p>
        </div>
        <div>
            <p>
                Select a file to upload:
                <asp:FileUpload ID="fileuploadPicture"
                                    runat="server" />
            </p>
        </div>
        <div>
            <asp:Button ID="btnUploadPicture" runat="server"
                            Text="Upload Picture" />
            <asp:Label ID="lUploadMsg" runat="server"/>
        </div>
    </div>
    </form>
</body>
</html>
```

The following is the code behind for the `UploadOrderPictures.aspx`:

```
Imports Microsoft.WindowsAzure
Imports Microsoft.WindowsAzure.StorageClient
Imports Microsoft.WindowsAzure.ServiceRuntime
Imports System.Data.SqlClient

Partial Public Class UploadOrderPicture
    Inherits System.Web.UI.Page

    Protected Sub Page_Load(ByVal sender As Object,
                    ByVal e As System.EventArgs) Handles Me.Load
        Try
            If Not Page.IsPostBack Then
                Me.LoadOrdersInProduction()
            End If

        Catch ex As Exception
            lUploadMsg.Text = "Error: " & ex.Message()
        End Try

    End Sub

    Private Sub LoadOrdersInProduction()
```

```vb
    Try
        Dim _connStr As String =
                    ConfigurationManager.ConnectionStrings
                    ("portal").ConnectionString
        Dim _SQLcon As New SqlConnection(_connStr)
        Dim _SQLcmd As New SqlCommand()

        _SQLcon.Open()

        With _SQLcmd
            .CommandText = "GetOrdersInProduction"
            .CommandType = CommandType.StoredProcedure
            .Connection = _SQLcon
        End With
        ddlOrdersInProduction.DataSource =
                            _SQLcmd.ExecuteReader()
        ddlOrdersInProduction.DataTextField = "CustomerPO"
        ddlOrdersInProduction.DataValueField = "OrderHeaderID"
        ddlOrdersInProduction.DataBind()
        ddlOrdersInProduction.Items.
        Insert(0, New ListItem("Choose an order...", "0"))
    Catch ex As Exception
        lUploadMsg.Text = "Error: " & ex.Message()
    End Try

End Sub


Protected Sub btnUploadPicture_Click(ByVal sender As Object,
        ByVal e As EventArgs) Handles btnUploadPicture.Click
    If fileuploadPicture.HasFile Then
        Try
            Dim _pictureID As String = Guid.NewGuid.ToString()
            Me.SaveImageToBlobStorage(ddlOrdersInProduction.
SelectedItem.ToString, _pictureID, fileuploadPicture.FileName, _
                                fileuploadPicture.PostedFile.
ContentType, fileuploadPicture.FileBytes)
            Me.InsertOrderPictureInTable
            (ddlOrdersInProduction.SelectedValue, _pictureID)
            lUploadMsg.Text =
                        "The picture has been loaded
                        into Blob Storage successfully."
        Catch ex As Exception
            lUploadMsg.Text = "Error: " & ex.Message()
        End Try
    Else
```

```
                    lUploadMsg.Text = "You must select a file to upload."
                End If

        End Sub


        ''' <summary>
        ''' This routine will insert the picture into Blob Storage
        ''' </summary>
        ''' <param name="sOrderNo"></param>
        ''' <param name="sId"></param>
        ''' <param name="sFileName"></param>
        ''' <param name="sContentType"></param>
        ''' <param name="bData"></param>
        ''' <remarks></remarks>
        Private Sub SaveImageToBlobStorage(ByVal sOrderNo As String,
                                    ByVal sId As String,
                                    ByVal sFileName As String, _
                                    ByVal sContentType As String,
                                    ByVal bData As Byte())
            Try
                'Make sure the container exists in
                 Blob Storage and get the Blob reference
                Me.CreateContainerIfNotExists(sOrderNo)
                Dim _blob =
                Me.GetContainer(sOrderNo).GetBlobReference(sId)

                'Set the Blob Content Type
                _blob.Properties.ContentType = sContentType

                'Set Metadata Values
                Dim _metadata = New NameValueCollection()
                _metadata("Uploaded") = Date.Now


                'Upload Metadata for Blob, then upload the Blob itself
                _blob.Metadata.Add(_metadata)
                _blob.UploadByteArray(bData)
            Catch ex As Exception
                lUploadMsg.Text = "Error: " & ex.Message()
            End Try

        End Sub

        ''' <summary>
```

```vb
''' This routine creates the container
    in Blob Storage if it does not exist
''' and sets the permissions to Public Access
''' </summary>
''' <param name="sContainer"></param>
''' <remarks></remarks>
Private Sub CreateContainerIfNotExists
(ByVal sContainer As String)
    Try
        Dim _container = GetContainer(sContainer)
        _container.CreateIfNotExist()

        Dim _permissions = _container.GetPermissions()
        _permissions.PublicAccess =
         BlobContainerPublicAccessType.Container
        _container.SetPermissions(_permissions)
    Catch ex As Exception
        lUploadMsg.Text = "Error: " & ex.Message()
    End Try
End Sub


''' <summary>
''' This function retrieves the Container Reference
''' </summary>
''' <param name="sContainer"></param>
''' <returns></returns>
''' <remarks></remarks>
Private Function GetContainer(ByVal sContainer As String)
                          As CloudBlobContainer
    Try
        Dim _account =
        CloudStorageAccount.DevelopmentStorageAccount()
        Dim _client = _account.CreateCloudBlobClient()

        Return _client.GetContainerReference(sContainer)

    Catch ex As Exception
        Throw New Exception("Error: " & ex.Message())
    End Try
End Function


''' <summary>
''' This routine will add the record to the OrderPictures table
''' </summary>
''' <param name="iOrderHeaderID"></param>
```

```
'''  <param name="sPictureFile"></param>
'''  <remarks></remarks>
Private Sub InsertOrderPictureInTable
        (ByVal iOrderHeaderID As Integer,
         ByVal sPictureFile As String)
    Try
        Dim _connStr As String =
        ConfigurationManager.ConnectionStrings
        ("portal").ConnectionString
        Dim _SQLcon As New SqlConnection(_connStr)
        Dim _SQLcmd As New SqlCommand()

        _SQLcon.Open()

        With _SQLcmd
            .CommandText = "NewOrderPicture"
            .CommandType = CommandType.StoredProcedure
            .Connection = _SQLcon
            .Parameters.AddWithValue
            ("@OrderHeaderID", iOrderHeaderID)
            .Parameters.AddWithValue
            ("@PictureFile", sPictureFile)
            .ExecuteNonQuery()
        End With
    Catch ex As Exception
        lUploadMsg.Text = ex.Message()
    End Try
End Sub

End Class
```

The following is the `ViewOrders.aspx` HTML file code:

```
<%@ Page Language="vb" AutoEventWireup="false" CodeBehind="ViewOrders.
aspx.vb" Inherits="WebRole1.ViewOrders" %>

<!DOCTYPE html PUBLIC "-//W3C//DTD XHTML 1.0 Transitional//EN"
"http://www.w3.org/TR/xhtml1/DTD/xhtml1-transitional.dtd">
<html xmlns="http://www.w3.org/1999/xhtml">
<head runat="server">
    <title></title>
</head>
<body>
    <form id="form1" runat="server">
    <div>
        <h1>
```

```
        View Orders Page</h1>
    <p>
        This is where we view our order
        status and any picture updates for an order.</p>
</div>
<div>
    <asp:Label ID="lMessage" runat="server" />
    <p>
        Customer PO:
        <asp:DropDownList ID="ddlOrders"
        runat="server" AutoPostBack="true" />
        Hint: Order must be "In Production"
        status to view picture updates.
    </p>
    <h3>
        Order Status:
    </h3>
    <p>
        The selected order is currently in status:
        <asp:Label ID="lOrderStatus" runat="server" />
    </p>
</div>
<div>
<h3>
    Uploaded Pictures for the selected order:
</h3>
    <asp:ListView ID="lstVwOrderPictures"
    runat="server" OnItemDataBound="AfterBlobDataBinding">
        <LayoutTemplate>
            <asp:PlaceHolder ID="itemPlaceHolder" runat="server" />
        </LayoutTemplate>
        <EmptyDataTemplate>
            <p>
                No pictures have yet been
                uploaded for this order. Please check back later.
            </p>
        </EmptyDataTemplate>
        <ItemTemplate>
            <div>
                <ul>
                    <asp:Repeater ID="metadataRepeater"
                    runat="server">
                        <ItemTemplate>
                            <li>
```

```
                              <%# Eval("Name") %>
                              -
                              <%#Eval("Value")%></li>
                         </ItemTemplate>
                    </asp:Repeater>
               </ul>
               <img src="<%# Eval("Uri") %>"
               alt="<%# Eval("Uri") %>" />
          </div>
     </ItemTemplate>
   </asp:ListView>
 </div>
 </form>
</body>
</html>
```

The following is the code behind for `ViewOrders.aspx`:

```vb
Imports Microsoft.WindowsAzure
Imports Microsoft.WindowsAzure.StorageClient
Imports Microsoft.WindowsAzure.ServiceRuntime
Imports System.Data.SqlClient

Partial Public Class ViewOrders
    Inherits System.Web.UI.Page

    Protected Sub Page_Load(ByVal sender As Object,
                    ByVal e As System.EventArgs) Handles Me.Load
        If Not Page.IsPostBack Then
            Me.LoadOrders()
        End If

        Me.ShowOrderPictures(ddlOrders.SelectedItem.ToString)
        Me.GetOrderStatusForSelectedOrder(ddlOrders.SelectedValue)
    End Sub

    Private Sub LoadOrders()
        Try
            Dim _connStr As String =
                    ConfigurationManager.ConnectionStrings
                    ("portal").ConnectionString
            Dim _SQLcon As New SqlConnection(_connStr)
            Dim _SQLcmd As New SqlCommand()

            _SQLcon.Open()
```

```vb
        With _SQLcmd
            .CommandText = "GetOrders"
            .CommandType = CommandType.StoredProcedure
            .Connection = _SQLcon
        End With
        ddlOrders.DataSource = _SQLcmd.ExecuteReader()
        ddlOrders.DataTextField = "CustomerPO"
        ddlOrders.DataValueField = "OrderHeaderID"
        ddlOrders.DataBind()
        ddlOrders.Items.Insert
        (0, New ListItem("Choose an order...", "0"))
    Catch ex As Exception
        lMessage.Text = "Error: " & ex.Message()
    End Try

End Sub


Private Sub GetOrderStatusForSelectedOrder
(ByVal iOrderHeaderID As Integer)
    Try
        Dim _connStr As String =
            ConfigurationManager.ConnectionStrings
            ("portal").ConnectionString
        Dim _SQLcon As New SqlConnection(_connStr)
        Dim _SQLcmd As New SqlCommand()


        _SQLcon.Open()

        With _SQLcmd
            .CommandText = "GetOrderStatusForOrderHeaderID"
            .CommandType = CommandType.StoredProcedure
            .Connection = _SQLcon
            .Parameters.AddWithValue
            ("@OrderHeaderID", iOrderHeaderID)
        End With
        lOrderStatus.Text =
                    _SQLcmd.ExecuteScalar()
    Catch ex As Exception
        lMessage.Text = ex.Message()
    End Try
End Sub


''' <summary>
''' This routine retrieves the pictures from
    Blob Storage for an order
```

```vb
''' and databinds them to the ListView "lstVwOrderPictures"
''' </summary>
''' <param name="sOrder"></param>
''' <remarks></remarks>
Private Sub ShowOrderPictures(ByVal sOrder As String)
    Dim _options As BlobRequestOptions = New BlobRequestOptions()
    _options.BlobListingDetails = BlobListingDetails.All
    _options.UseFlatBlobListing = True

    If ddlOrders.SelectedValue <> 0 Then
        Me.CreateContainerIfNotExists(sOrder)
        lstVwOrderPictures.DataSource =
        Me.GetContainer(sOrder).ListBlobs(_options)
        lstVwOrderPictures.DataBind()
    End If

End Sub


''' <summary>
''' This routine creates the container in
    Blob Storage if it does not exist
''' and sets the permissions to Public Access
''' </summary>
''' <param name="sContainer"></param>
''' <remarks></remarks>
Private Sub CreateContainerIfNotExists
        (ByVal sContainer As String)
    Try
        Dim _container = GetContainer(sContainer)
        _container.CreateIfNotExist()

        Dim _permissions = _container.GetPermissions()
        _permissions.PublicAccess =
        BlobContainerPublicAccessType.Container
        _container.SetPermissions(_permissions)
    Catch ex As Exception
        lMessage.Text = "Error: " & ex.Message()
    End Try
End Sub

''' <summary>
''' This function retrieves the Container Reference
''' </summary>
''' <param name="sContainer"></param>
''' <returns></returns>
```

```vbnet
''' <remarks></remarks>
Private Function GetContainer
        (ByVal sContainer As String) As CloudBlobContainer
    Try
        Dim _account =
        CloudStorageAccount.DevelopmentStorageAccount()
        Dim _client = _account.CreateCloudBlobClient()

        Return _client.GetContainerReference(sContainer)

    Catch ex As Exception
        Throw New Exception("Error: " & ex.Message())
    End Try
End Function


''' <summary>
''' This routine is called after the
    blob has been databound to the ListView "lstVwOrderPictures"
''' and sets the metadata to the repeater (Uploaded Date & Time)
''' </summary>
''' <param name="sender"></param>
''' <param name="e"></param>
''' <remarks></remarks>
Protected Sub AfterBlobDataBinding
(ByVal sender As Object, ByVal e As ListViewItemEventArgs)
    If e.Item.ItemType = ListViewItemType.DataItem Then
        Dim _metadataRepeater =
        TryCast(e.Item.FindControl("metadataRepeater"), Repeater)
        Dim _blob = TryCast(DirectCast((e.Item),
        ListViewDataItem).DataItem, CloudBlob)

        If _metadataRepeater IsNot Nothing Then
            'bind to metadata
            _metadataRepeater.DataSource = From _key In
            _blob.Metadata.AllKeys _
                Select New With {.Name = _key, .Value =
                _blob.Metadata.Get(_key)}
            _metadataRepeater.DataBind()
        End If
    End If
End Sub
End Class
```

Our `Web.config` has only one addition beyond the original generated code for the trace listener — the connection string, `portal`, has been added to the connection strings section of the file.

```
<configuration>
    <connectionStrings>
            <add name="portal"
            connectionString="server=(local)\SQLEXPRESS;
            database=portal;uid=Portal;pwd=P@ssw0rd"/>
    </connectionStrings>
```

Our web role is now complete and should look like this:

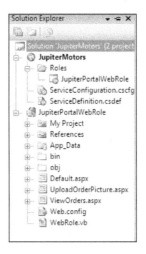

Summary

Our Jupiter Motors web role is now complete. We can now upload pictures into Blob Storage via the UploadOrderPicture.aspx page, and view the orders, statuses for orders, and any uploaded pictures via the ViewOrders.aspx page. In the next chapter, we will tackle Windows Communication Foundation (WCF) in our Windows Azure application!

10
Web Services and Azure

Technically, web services are part of the web role, but their use and development are so distinctly different than web forms that we'll look at these separately. The web services themselves can be written in any language supported by Azure, but utilizing the Windows Communication Foundation (WCF) libraries in .NET greatly simplifies the development of web services. The simple storage services have their own REST API and client library developed, but if we want to add data into SQL Azure, we'll have to create our own web services.

In this chapter, we'll:

- Gain an overview of WCF services
- Build the WCF service for the Jupiter Motors portal

Web services and WCF

A web service is not one single entity and consists of three distinct parts:

- An **endpoint**, which is the URL (and related information) where client applications will find our service
- A **host environment**, which in our case will be Azure
- A **service class**, which is the code that implements the methods called by the client application

A web service endpoint is more than just a URL. An endpoint also includes:

- The bindings, or communication and security protocols
- The contract (or promise) that certain methods exist, how these methods should be called, and what the data will look like when returned

A simple way to remember the components of an endpoint is *A/B/C*, that is, *address/bindings/contract*.

Web services can fill many roles in our Azure applications—from serving as a simple way to place messages into a queue, to being a complete replacement for a data access layer in a web application (also known as a Service Oriented Architecture or SOA). In Azure, web services serve as HTTP/HTTPS endpoints, which can be accessed by any application that supports REST, regardless of language or operating system.

The intrinsic web services libraries in .NET are called **Windows Communication Foundation (WCF)**. As WCF is designed specifically for programming web services, it's referred to as a *service-oriented programming model*. We are not limited to using WCF libraries in Azure development, but we expect it to be a popular choice for constructing web services being part of the .NET framework. A complete introduction to WCF can be found at `http://msdn.microsoft.com/en-us/netframework/aa663324.aspx`.

When adding WCF services to an Azure web role, we can either create a separate web role instance, or add the web services to an existing web role. Using separate instances allows us to scale the web services independently of the web forms, but multiple instances increase our operating costs. Separate instances also allow us to use different technologies for each Azure instance; for example, the web form may be written in PHP and hosted on Apache, while the web services may be written in Java and hosted using Tomcat. Using the same instance helps keep our costs much lower, but in that case we have to scale both the web forms and the web services together. Depending on our application's architecture, this may not be desirable.

Securing WCF

Stored data are only as secure as the application used for accessing it. The Internet is stateless, and REST has no sense of security, so security information must be passed as part of the data in each request. If the credentials are not encrypted, then all requests should be forced to use HTTPS. If we control the consuming client applications, we can also control the encryption of the user credentials. Otherwise, our only choice may be to use clear text credentials via HTTPS.

For an application with a wide or uncontrolled distribution (like most commercial applications want to be), or if we are to support a number of home-brewed applications, the authorization information must be unique to the user. Part of the behind-the-services code should check to see if the user making the request can be authenticated, and if the user is authorized to perform the action. This adds additional coding overhead, but it's easier to plan for this up front.

There are a number of ways to secure web services—from using HTTPS and passing credentials with each request, to using authentication tokens in each request. As it happens, using authentication tokens is part of the AppFabric Access Control, and we'll look more into the security for WCF when we dive deeper into Access Control.

Jupiter Motors web service

In our corporate portal for Jupiter Motors, we included a design for a client application, which our delivery personnel will use to update the status of an order and to decide which customers will accept delivery of their vehicle. For accounting and insurance reasons, the order status needs to be updated immediately after a customer accepts their vehicle. To do so, the client application will call a web service to update the order status as soon as the **Accepted** button is clicked. Our WCF service is interconnected to other parts of our Jupiter Motors application, so we won't see it completely in action until it all comes together. In the meantime, it will seem like we're developing blind. In reality, all the components would probably be developed and tested simultaneously, but the structure of a book makes that difficult.

Creating a new WCF service web role

When creating a web service, we have a choice to add the web service to an existing web role, or create a new web role. This helps us deploy and maintain our website application separately from our web services. And in order for us to scale the web role independently from the worker role, we'll create our web service in a role separate from our web application. Creating a new WCF service web role is very simple—Visual Studio will do the "hard work" for us and allow us to start coding our services.

First, open the `JupiterMotors` project. Create the new web role by right-clicking on the `Roles` folder in our project, choosing **Add**, and then select the **New Web Role Project...** option.

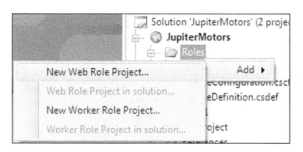

When we do this, we will be asked what type of web role we want to create. We will choose a WCF Service Web Role, call it `JupiterMotorsWCFRole`, and click on the **Add** button. Because different services must have unique names in our project, a good naming convention to use is the project name concatenated with the type of role. This makes the different roles and instances easily discernable, and complies with the unique naming requirement.

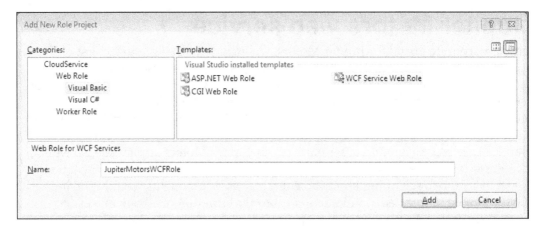

This is where Visual Studio does its magic. It creates the new role in the cloud project, creates a new web role for our WCF web services, and creates some template code for us. The template service created is called "Service1". You will see both, a `Service1.svc` file as well as an `IService1.vb` file. Also, a `web.config` file (as we would expect to see in any web role) is created in the web role and is already wired up for our Service1 web service. All of the generated code is very helpful if you are learning WCF web services.

This is what we should see once Visual Studio finishes creating the new project:

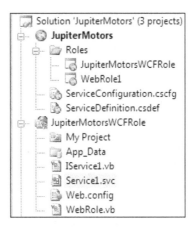

We are going to start afresh with our own services — we can delete `Service1.svc` and `IService1.vb`. Also, in the `web.config` file, the following boilerplate code can be deleted (we'll add our own code as needed):

```xml
<system.serviceModel>
  <services>
    <service name="JupiterMotorsWCFRole.Service1"
                behaviorConfiguration="JupiterMotorsWCFRole.
                Service1Behavior">
      <!-- Service Endpoints -->
      <endpoint address="" binding="basicHttpBinding"
              contract="JupiterMotorsWCFRole.IService1">
        <!--
            Upon deployment, the following identity
            element should be removed or replaced to reflect the
            identity under which the deployed service runs.
            If removed, WCF will infer an appropriate identity
            automatically.
        -->
        <identity>
          <dns value="localhost"/>
        </identity>
      </endpoint>
      <endpoint address="mex" binding="mexHttpBinding"
                      contract="IMetadataExchange"/>
    </service>
  </services>
  <behaviors>
    <serviceBehaviors>
      <behavior name="JupiterMotorsWCFRole.Service1Behavior">
        <!-- To avoid disclosing metadata information,
            set the value below to false and remove the
            metadata endpoint above before deployment -->
        <serviceMetadata httpGetEnabled="true"/>
        <!-- To receive exception details in faults for debugging
              purposes, set the value below to true.
              Set to false before deployment to avoid
              disclosing exception information -->
        <serviceDebug includeExceptionDetailInFaults="false"/>
      </behavior>
    </serviceBehaviors>
  </behaviors>
</system.serviceModel>
```

Let's now add a WCF service to the `JupiterMotorsWCFRole` project. To do so, right-click on the project, then **Add**, and select the **New Item...** option.

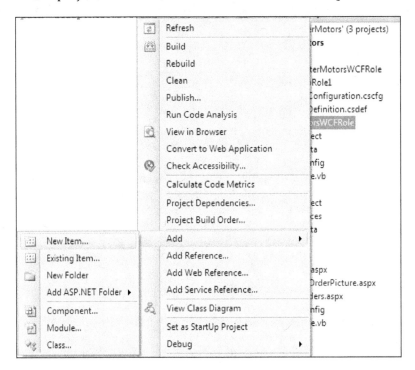

We now choose a WCF service and will name it as `ERPService.svc`:

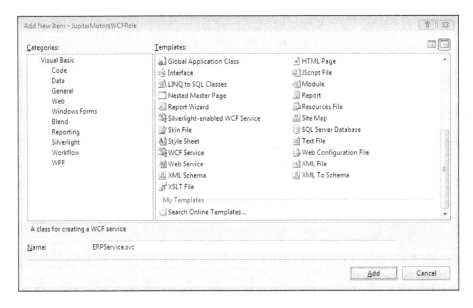

Just like the generated code when we created the web role, ERPService.svc as well as IERPService.vb files were created for us, and these are now wired into the web.config file. There is some generated code in the ERPService.svc and IERPService.vb files, but we will replace this with our code in the next section. When we create a web service, the actual service class is created with the name we specify. Additionally, an interface class is automatically created. We can specify the name for the class; however, being an interface class, it will always have its name beginning with letter I. This is a special type of interface class, called a service contract. The service contract provides a description of what methods and return types are available in our web service.

Our WCF web services

Our WCF web service is going to expose two functions to return data to the client and one routine to add a message to the queue when an order status is updated on the client.

ERP service interface—IERPService.vb

These following functions and routines will be exposed when the service is called from the client. This is our code in our IERPService.vb file, in the WCFWebService1 role:

```
Imports System.ServiceModel

' NOTE: If you change the class name "IERPService" here, you must also
update the reference to "IERPService" in Web.config.
<ServiceContract()> _
Public Interface IERPService

    <OperationContract()> _
    Function LoadStartupData() As DataSet

    <OperationContract()> _
    Function GetOrderStatusForOrder(ByVal iOrderHeaderID As Integer)
As String

    <OperationContract()> _
    Sub AddOrderStatusUpdateToQueue(ByVal iOrderHeaderID As Integer,
ByVal iOrderStatusID As Integer)

    <DataContract()> _
    Class OrderStatus
```

```
        Private statusName_value As String

        <DataMember()> _
        Public Property StatusName() As String
                Get
                        Return statusName_value
                End Get
                Set(ByVal value As String)
                        statusName_value = value
                End Set
        End Property

    End Class

  End Interface
```

Now that we've created our interface, we can see it looks very similar to a traditional interface, but the class and methods are decorated with contract attributes.

Service Contract

As we mentioned above, a Service Contract is a class-level attribute. The Service Contract is the top level of the service definition, and encapsulates both the operations and data. Just as methods and properties are children of a class, Operation Contracts and Data Contracts are children of a Service Contract.

Operation Contract

The Operation Contract specifies the methods and the method signatures that the web service client can call. Not all methods in the Service Contract need to be labelled as Operation Contracts. Web services may use any number of helper methods to support the publicly accessible ones.

Data Contract

The Data Contract describes how the returned data will be serialized or deserialized. A Data Contract is a separate class in our interface; the data elements are properties with the `<DataMember()>` attribute.

If we are returning a simple data structure—say a list of names—we do not necessarily need to establish a Data Contract. However, using a Data Contract is recommended as a best practice.

For more advanced data types, even something as basic as a list of name-value pairs, we need to include a Data Contract. We'll use a Data Contract to return the status of an order.

For some additional information on Service, Operation, and Data Contracts, visit `http://msdn.microsoft.com/en-us/library/system.servicemodel.servicecontractattribute.aspx`. Data Contracts in particular are covered in greater depth at `http://msdn.microsoft.com/en-us/library/ms733127.aspx`.

Using ADO.NET datasets

As ADO.NET datasets are serializable objects, it is possible to skip using a Data Contract, and allow WCF to serialize a dataset. The one caveat is that we need to make sure our client is .NET based so that it can deserialize the dataset properly. An advantage ADO.NET datasets have is returning multiple recordsets in the same method call. This can speed up performance by reducing the number of server requests. We'll use this technique to load our client application's startup data.

ERP service implementation—ERPService. svc.vb

Here are the actual functions and routines that will be executed when called from the client. We can keep both the functions and routines directly linked to the service calls (these are marked with `Implements IERPService.[function or routine name]`) and also other functions and routines that can be called (just like any other class):

```vb
Imports System.Data.SqlClient
Imports Microsoft.WindowsAzure
Imports Microsoft.WindowsAzure.StorageClient
Imports Microsoft.WindowsAzure.ServiceRuntime


' NOTE: If you change the class name "ERPService" here, you must
also update the reference to "ERPService" in Web.config and in the
associated .svc file.
Public Class ERPService
    Implements IERPService
```

LoadStartupData service function

This function returns a dataset to the client with two different DataTables—one is the list of orders not yet complete and the other is a list of order statuses. These will be databound to list boxes in the client ERP application we'll create in *Chapter 12*.

```
Private Function LoadStartupData() As DataSet Implements
                IERPService.LoadStartupData
    Dim _dataSet As New DataSet

    _dataSet = GetOrdersNotComplete(_dataSet)
    _dataSet = GetOrderStatuses(_dataSet)


    Return _dataSet

End Function
```

GetOrderStatusForOrder service function

This function will accept an Order Header ID and return the status for that particular order. This will be used to show the order status for a selected order, in a list box, in our client ERP application.

```
Private Function GetOrderStatusForOrder(ByVal iOrderHeaderID As
                Integer) As String Implements
                IERPService.GetOrderStatusForOrder
    Dim _connStr As String =
                ConfigurationManager.ConnectionStrings
                ("portal").ConnectionString
    Dim _SQLcon As New SqlConnection(_connStr)
    Dim _SQLcmd As New SqlCommand()

    _SQLcon.Open()

    With _SQLcmd
        .CommandText = "GetOrderStatusForOrderHeaderID"
        .CommandType = CommandType.StoredProcedure
        .Connection = _SQLcon
        .Parameters.AddWithValue
                ("@orderHeaderID", iOrderHeaderID)
    End With

    Return _SQLcmd.ExecuteScalar().ToString

End Function
```

AddOrderStatusUpdateToQueue service function

The following function will take the Order Header ID for a selected order, the Order Status ID for a selected status, and add a message to our queue for our worker role to pick up and update the order (which we will see in the next chapter).

```
Private Sub AddOrderStatusUpdateToQueue(ByVal iOrderHeaderID As
    Integer, ByVal iOrderStatusID As Integer)
    Implements IERPService.AddOrderStatusUpdateToQueue
Dim _account =
    CloudStorageAccount.DevelopmentStorageAccount()
Dim _client = _account.CreateCloudQueueClient()

Dim _queue As CloudQueue =
    _client.GetQueueReference("orderupdatequeue")

_queue.CreateIfNotExist()

Dim _msg As New CloudQueueMessage
    (iOrderHeaderID & "," & iOrderStatusID)
_queue.AddMessage(_msg)

End Sub
```

GetOrdersNotComplete, GetOrderStatuses, and CreateDataSetFromDataReader class functions

The following functions will do the work of retrieving data and packaging the DataTables into the DataSet to return to the client. These functions will be called by the service functions we looked at in the previous section. They do not implement a service function.

```
Private Function GetOrdersNotComplete
    (ByVal dsLoadData As DataSet) As DataSet
Dim _connStr As String =
    ConfigurationManager.ConnectionStrings
    ("portal").ConnectionString
Dim _SQLcon As New SqlConnection(_connStr)
Dim _SQLcmd As New SqlCommand()

_SQLcon.Open()

With _SQLcmd
    .CommandText = "GetOrdersNotComplete"
    .CommandType = CommandType.StoredProcedure
```

```
                    .Connection = _SQLcon
            End With

            dsLoadData = CreateDataSetFromDataReader
                        (_SQLcmd.ExecuteReader(),
                        dsLoadData, "OrdersNotComplete")

            Return dsLoadData

    End Function

    Private Function GetOrderStatuses
            (ByVal dsLoadData As DataSet) As DataSet

        Dim _connStr As String =
            ConfigurationManager.ConnectionStrings
            ("portal").ConnectionString
        Dim _SQLcon As New SqlConnection(_connStr)
        Dim _SQLcmd As New SqlCommand()

        _SQLcon.Open()

        With _SQLcmd
            .CommandText = "GetOrderStatuses"
            .CommandType = CommandType.StoredProcedure
            .Connection = _SQLcon
        End With

        dsLoadData = CreateDataSetFromDataReader
                    (_SQLcmd.ExecuteReader(),
                    dsLoadData, "OrderStatuses")

        Return dsLoadData
    End Function


    Private Function CreateDataSetFromDataReader
            (ByVal drReader As SqlDataReader,
            ByVal dsDataSet As DataSet, ByVal
            sTableName As String) As DataSet
        Do
            Dim _schemaTable As DataTable = drReader.GetSchemaTable()
            Dim _dataTable As New DataTable()

            If _schemaTable IsNot Nothing Then
                'The SqlDataReader returned results
```

```vb
        'Set the DataTable Name to reference from DataSet
        _dataTable.TableName = sTableName

        For i As Integer = 0 To _schemaTable.Rows.Count - 1
            Dim _dataRow As DataRow = _schemaTable.Rows(i)
            'Create the column names
            Dim _columnName As String =
                _dataRow("ColumnName").ToString

            'Set the column type
            Dim _column As New DataColumn
                (_columnName, DirectCast
                (_dataRow("DataType"), Type))
            _dataTable.Columns.Add(_column)
        Next

        'Add DataTable to DataSet
        dsDataSet.Tables.Add(_dataTable)

        'Fill DataTable with results from SqlDataReader
        While drReader.Read()
            Dim _dataRow As DataRow = _dataTable.NewRow()

            For i As Integer = 0 To drReader.FieldCount - 1
                _dataRow(i) = drReader.GetValue(i)
            Next

            _dataTable.Rows.Add(_dataRow)
        End While
      End If
    Loop While drReader.NextResult()
    Return dsDataSet
  End Function

End Class
```

DataTable "gotcha"

Our original plan was to make two different calls to the web service for the databinding of the list boxes in Chapter 12, and passing back the lists as a DataTable to the client. The beauty of WCF services is that they can accept and return a wide variety of serializable objects. At the time of writing, DataTables have been made serializable but are not yet working through WCF, though DataSets are. This is why we opted to package the DataTables into a DataSet and pass it back to the client.

There are advantages and disadvantages to doing it this way. There are two major advantages to this:

- We need to give only one call to the client with only one returned object to use

- Client application speed is greater with only one call

The disadvantage to this is that the total size of a DataSet with one DataTable is much bigger than the size of just the DataTable itself. The increased size could take longer to transfer and also use more bandwidth. Our example is a very small set of data; however, the DataSets in a real-life enterprise application could be a lot bigger.

Web Service Definition Language (WSDL) "gotcha"

As we learned earlier in the book, the Windows Azure development fabric runs on localhost, port 81 (or `http://localhost:81` as you would see it in your Internet browser). If you've ever dealt with web services, the following information displayed on the page in your internet browser will look familiar:

ERPService Service

You have created a service.

To test this service, you will need to create a client and use it to call the service. You can do this using the svcutil.exe tool from the command line with the following syntax:

```
svcutil.exe http://localhost:1289/ERPService.svc?wsdl
```

This will generate a configuration file and a code file that contains the client class. Add the two files to your client application and use the generated client class to call the Service. For example:

Great news! Our service seems to be running fine! Or is it? Look at the link for the service to get the WSDL: `http://localhost:1289/ERPService.svc?wsdl` That's not the port we were expecting. If you follow the instructions on the page to test it using the `svcutil.exe`, we get the following error:

Error: Cannot obtain Metadata from http://localhost:1289/ERPService.svc. If this is a Windows (R) Communication Foundation service to which you have access, please check that you have enabled metadata publishing at the specified address. For help enabling metadata publishing, please refer to the MSDN documentation at http://go.microsoft.com/fwlink/?LinkId=65455.WS-Metadata Exchange Error URI: http://localhost:1289/ERPService.svc Metadata contains a reference that cannot be resolved: 'http://localhost:1289/ERPService.svc'. There was no endpoint listening at http://localhost:1289/ERPService.svc that could accept the message. This is often caused by an incorrect address or SOAP action. See InnerException, if present, for more details. The remote server returned an error: (400) Bad Request.HTTP GET Error URI: http://localhost:1289/ERPService.svc There was an error downloading 'http://localhost:1289/ERPService.svc'. The request failed with HTTP status 400: Bad Request.

It looks like there is a metadata error, but we know we have metadata publishing enabled as the page is able to display the publishing instructions. After digging around for the answer, the problem was found. The `schemaLocation` reference was incorrect in the WSDL. Microsoft has released a hotfix to correct this (one for Vista and Server 2008, and the other for Windows 7):

- **Windows Vista and Server 2008**: Download KB971842. To do this, go to `http://support.microsoft.com/kb/971842` for information and to download.

- **Windows 7**: Download KB981002. To do so, go to `http://support.microsoft.com/kb/981002` for information and to download.

Once downloaded and installed, the address to get the WSDL stays the same; however, the `schemaLocation` reference is corrected and all is fine once again! Now that we're able to generate the WSDL in our local development environment, we're set to develop our client application.

Summary

In this chapter, we looked briefly at web services and WCF, and how they fit into an Azure project. We then developed our WCF classes in a new web role. Because our web service is interconnected to other parts of the Jupiter Motors portal project, there is additional work to be done before we can see the web services in action. Web services are very powerful, and we're only scratching the surface, so if additional samples are desired, a good resource is available at `http://code.msdn.microsoft.com/wcfazure`.

11
Worker Roles

Besides the web role, the Compute Service's other role is the **Worker Role**. Worker roles are used for behind-the-scenes processing functions, and can also serve as HTTP/HTTPS/TCP endpoints. Although they don't function in exactly the same way, it's easy to think of worker roles as being similar to the services on our local machines.

In this chapter, we'll cover:

- Worker role internals
- Uses for worker roles
- Externally facing worker roles
- Thread-pool pattern
- Building the Jupiter Motors worker role

Worker role internals

Building worker roles is fairly simple—they are just class libraries that inherit from the Microsoft.ServiceHosting.ServiceRuntime.RoleEntryPoint class. Worker roles are automatically started when their host instance is started. During startup, code in the OnStart() method is executed. The OnStart() method returns a Boolean value. If OnStart() returns true, the role is started and the Run() method is called, whereas if OnStart() returns false, the role is stopped.

Our worker tasks should be coded in the Run() method, and we should not return from the Run() method. If we do, Azure will restart the worker role. Instead, and despite our best instincts, the code in the Run() method should be enclosed inside an infinite loop. The way to stop a worker role is to stop the host instance. For this reason, worker roles that need to function independently should all be separated into individual instances.

When our worker role instance is being shut down by Azure, the `OnStop()` method is called. We can add cleanup code to this method if necessary, or just a return statement. `OnStop()` is not called in the event of application or hardware failure. The Azure Fabric will wait for 20 seconds to receive a return code. If more than 20 seconds of time elapses, the role will be killed regardless of its status or place in executing the code.

We can use any .NET language to develop worker roles. This is different from web roles, which can be programmed in .NET and non-.NET languages. Even if we're using Azure to host a server for a non-.NET language, there is still a little bit of plumbing that needs to be done in a .NET language. There are "solution accelerators" and examples for plumbing most of the major alternative web servers.

Uses of worker roles

Worker roles can be used to perform a variety of functions. Some of the uses of worker roles include:

- Processing messages contained in Queue Storage (thread-pool pattern)
- Retrieving data from remote web services
- Hosting non-IIS servers such as Jetty (`http://blogs.msdn.com/b/dachou/archive/2010/03/21/run-java-with-jetty-in-windows-azure.aspx`), PHP (`http://blog.maartenballiauw.be/post/2010/04/08/Running-PHP-on-Windows-Azure.aspx`), and other web servers (`http://blog.smarx.com/posts/using-other-web-servers-on-windows-azure`)
- Serving as the TCP endpoint for FTP services (`http://blog.maartenballiauw.be/post/2010/03/15/Using-FTP-to-access-Windows-Azure-Blob-Storage.aspx`)
- Mounting an Azure CloudDrive VHD
- Accessing files on a CloudDrive VHD

Although worker roles can be used to host web servers for non-.NET languages, they can only be developed in .NET languages.

The uses of worker roles are limited only by the collective imagination of the Azure ecosystem. Microsoft has opened an Azure App Marketplace at `http://pinpoint.microsoft.com/en-US/windowsazure/resources`, where applications developed specifically for Azure are listed, most of which are worker roles or have worker role components. Before embarking on extensive worker role development, it might be a good idea to look through the App Marketplace.

Externally facing worker roles

One of the Azure features touted by Microsoft is that non-IIS servers can be used on Azure. Servers such as Tomcat and Jetty, as well as communications protocols such as FTP, have all been implemented on Azure. The mechanism by which these have been accomplished is externally facing worker roles. Worker roles can serve as TCP endpoints, and using the `System.Net.Sockets.TcpListener` class, we can create listeners for a number of protocols or ports. While IIS may be the primary web server on Azure, externally facing worker roles provide us with a great deal of options should we need to expand beyond IIS, or if we wish to utilize a non-.NET language.

Thread-pool pattern

In the thread-pool pattern (`http://en.wikipedia.org/wiki/Thread_pool_pattern`), work that needs to be done accumulates in a queue, and one or more threads process the work. As one unit or work is complete, the thread requests the next unit in the queue. When all the work is complete, the thread can rest or monitor until there is more work. Extending this pattern to Azure does not require a great deal of imagination, with Queue Storage serving as the work queue, and a worker role serving as the thread that processes work. Others have described this pattern as the work-queue pattern.

Managing worker roles

Azure is an elastic system, meaning resources can fairly easily scale up or shrink based on demand for those resources. Because the costs of Azure are based on resource utilization, there is a balance between cost and performance for our Azure applications; hence, managing roles is an essential part of a well-run Azure application.

So how do we know when to scale up a worker role? The answer depends largely on the overall system architecture. If we're experiencing high traffic, experiencing significant lags in processing time, and a queue is filling faster than it can be processed, it's probably time to increase the worker roles.

On the other hand, our system design may include a rate-limiting step to maintain system resources downstream. Or, our application may employ the singleton pattern to avoid data concurrency issues. In these cases, we'll have to look at other mechanisms to increase performance under high loads.

The initial number of instances for a particular role is specified using the `Instances` element in the `ServiceConfiguration.cscfg` file, as seen here:

```
<Role name="JupiterMotorsWorkerRole">
  <Instances count="1" />
  <ConfigurationSettings>
    <Setting name="DiagnosticsConnectionString"
                value="UseDevelopmentStorage=true" />
  </ConfigurationSettings>
</Role>
```

When we deploy our application, we can control the number of instances by adjusting the value of the `Instance` element. Should we need to scale up or down after the application is deployed, we can either change the number of instances in the Azure portal, or we can use the Service Management API (`http://msdn.microsoft.com/en-us/library/ee460799.aspx`). Changing the number of instances by editing the `ServiceConfiguration.cscfg` file is not recommended, as edits to this file will cause the roles is restart, similar to how editing the `web.config` file causes an ASP.NET web app to restart. Using the portal to increase the number of instances does not cause an application to restart, but if we decrease the number of instances, we do not have any control over which ones are shut down.

For a more automated solution, we can use another worker role to monitor the length of a queue, and if a queue becomes too backed-up, increase the number of worker roles. When the queue becomes depleted, the number of worker roles can be reduced by the monitoring role.

Best practices

When building worker roles, the standard best practices still apply — object-oriented design, reusable code, and so on.

An important additional practice is to add logging information. Worker roles operate invisibly, so they can be difficult to debug. All we may have are the symptoms of the malfunctioning role, with no indication of why the role is malfunctioning.

Another consideration in worker role design is limiting one worker role to one function. For instance, we shouldn't design worker roles to process work from more than one queue, even though it may be more cost-effective to do so. Limiting the number of functions a worker role performs allows us to scale only what is a bottleneck and not affect the processing of other data.

We also need to design for parallel operation. If we have multiple instances of the same worker role, we need to ensure they will not trip over each other and process the same data or miss other work.

When creating an externally facing worker role, we need to keep in mind that Azure is load balanced, and subsequent requests may not be processed by the same role instance. State needs to be maintained in a way that it can be accessed by one role instance on one request, and a different role instance on a different request. One method to achieve this is to serialize state information into blobs.

The Jupiter Motors worker role

When an RV is finished, a Jupiter Motors driver takes the RV from our factory to the customer. Because custom RVs can cost around US$400,000, and very high-end RVs can cost around US$1,000,000, it's important the customer takes ownership of the RV quickly. When a customer takes ownership of the vehicle, the vehicle is removed from Jupiter Motors' insurance and begins the billing cycles to the customer. In order to take ownership, the customer inspects the vehicle, and accepts delivery by filling out a small form in a custom application on the driver's laptop. The custom application calls our web service and updates the status of the order.

Rather than updating the database directly, the web service places a message in a queue to be processed by our worker role. We are not expecting a high degree of traffic through the web service, but the customer acceptance is a zero-failure process. The built-in failover mechanisms of a queue make it a very attractive way to add zero-failure with not too much extra work.

Building the Jupiter Motors worker role

Our Jupiter Motors worker role will take a message from our queue and will update the order status in our portal database. This process will occur with our local application simulating a handheld device with a connection to the Internet. The application will capture the OrderHeaderID and OrderStatusID from our portal database (via our WCF Web Service) and build a string for our queue message. The string will be in a simple format of [OrderHeaderID], [OrderStatusID]. Let's see how we can accomplish the task of reading this message and updating the database from our queue message.

First, we need to add a worker role to our project. We do this in the same manner that we added our WCF role in the previous chapter by right-clicking our roles folder in our `JupiterMotors` cloud application, choosing **Add**, and selecting the **New Worker Role Project...** option.

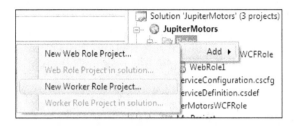

We're going to name our worker role as `JupiterMotorsWorkerRole`, as shown in the next screenshot:

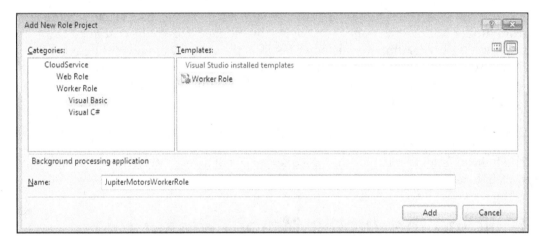

At this point, we can see that our worker role is created for us with an `app.config` file and a `WorkerRole.vb` file. A worker role executes much like a service in the background. There is no visual aspect of the worker role. It is exactly what the name claims—a worker. All of our code in the sample application will be placed in the `WorkerRole.vb` file. We are not limited to keeping all of our code though. We can create classes within the worker role project and split up the code if we want to. Our code for the Jupiter Motors worker role calls only one routine, so it is simple enough to keep within the `WorkerRole` class generated for us.

Notice that the `WorkerRole` class starts out with a routine `Public Overrides Sub Run()`. This is where our executable code will reside.

```vbnet
Imports System.Net
Imports System.Threading
Imports Microsoft.WindowsAzure.Diagnostics
Imports Microsoft.WindowsAzure.ServiceRuntime
Imports System.Data.SqlClient
Imports Microsoft.WindowsAzure
Imports Microsoft.WindowsAzure.StorageClient


Public Class WorkerRole
    Inherits RoleEntryPoint

  ' The Run() method is where the work is performed.
   We construct an infinite loop to ensure the role
  ' stays running.

    Public Overrides Sub Run()
        ' This is a sample implementation for
          JupiterMotorsWorkerRole. Replace with your logic.
        Trace.WriteLine("JupiterMotorsWorkerRole
        entry point called.", "Information")

            Dim _account =
            CloudStorageAccount.DevelopmentStorageAccount()
            Dim _client = _account.CreateCloudQueueClient()
            Dim _queue As CloudQueue =
            _client.GetQueueReference("orderupdatequeue")
            _queue.CreateIfNotExist()

        While (True)
            Thread.Sleep(10000)
            Trace.WriteLine("Working", "Information")

            'Gets a message from the queue
            Dim _msg As CloudQueueMessage = _queue.GetMessage()

            If Not _msg Is Nothing Then
                'Parse message to get the
                 orderHeaderId and orderStatusId
                Dim _orderHeaderId As Integer
                Dim _orderStatusId As Integer
                Dim _separatorPosition As Integer
```

```vbnet
                        Dim _messageLength As Integer

                        _messageLength = Len(_msg.AsString)
                        _separatorPosition = _msg.AsString.IndexOf(",") + 1

                        _orderHeaderId = Left(_msg.AsString,
                                    _messageLength - _separatorPosition)
                        _orderStatusId = Right(_msg.AsString,
                                    _messageLength - _separatorPosition)

                        'Call routine to update the order status
                        UpdateOrderStatus(_orderHeaderId,
                                        _orderStatusId)

                        'Delete the message from the queue
                            once order is updated
                        _queue.DeleteMessage(_msg)
                End If
                    _msg = nothing

            End While

    End Sub

' OnStart() runs only once, when
  the role is initially started.
  This is a good method to set up
' any diagnostic connections, connection limits, etc.

Public Overrides Function OnStart() As Boolean

        ' Set the maximum number of concurrent connections
        ServicePointManager.DefaultConnectionLimit = 12

        DiagnosticMonitor.Start("DiagnosticsConnectionString")

        ' For information on handling configuration changes
        ' see the MSDN topic at
          http://go.microsoft.com/fwlink/?LinkId=166357.
        AddHandler RoleEnvironment.Changing,
        AddressOf RoleEnvironmentChanging

        Return MyBase.OnStart()

    End Function
```

```vbnet
' RoleEnvironmentChanging is executed
  after configuration changes are made,
  but before the changes are applied.
' Setting e.Cancel=true allows the role
  to be recycled.  We can make the
  recycle conditional on some other
' value by modifying this method.

Private Sub RoleEnvironmentChanging
        (ByVal sender As Object, ByVal e As
         RoleEnvironmentChangingEventArgs)

    ' If a configuration setting is changing
    If (e.Changes.Any(Function(change)
        TypeOf change Is
        RoleEnvironmentConfigurationSettingChange))
    Then
        ' Set e.Cancel to true to restart this role instance
        e.Cancel = True
    End If

End Sub

Public Sub UpdateOrderStatus
        (ByVal iOrderHeaderId As Integer,
         ByVal iOrderStatusId As Integer)

    Dim _connStr As String = My.Settings.ConnectionString
    Dim _SQLcon As New SqlConnection(_connStr)
    Dim _SQLcmd As New SqlCommand()

    _SQLcon.Open()

    With _SQLcmd
        .CommandText = "UpdateOrderStatusForOrderHeaderID"
        .CommandType = CommandType.StoredProcedure
        .Connection = _SQLcon
        .Parameters.AddWithValue
          ("@OrderHeaderID", iOrderHeaderId)
        .Parameters.AddWithValue
          ("@OrderStatusID", iOrderStatusId)
        .ExecuteNonQuery()
    End With

End Sub

End Class
```

An important piece of the worker role is the `If Not _msg Is Nothing Then...` statement. This will make sure our code is executed only when there is a message in the queue that was picked up by the worker role. Without this, we would receive an **Object reference not set to an instance of an object** error. Other than that, the worker role is a very straightforward class to run executable code.

Summary

In this chapter, we looked at worker roles, which are the other main functionality provided by the Azure compute services. Similar to services on traditional operating systems, worker roles run in the background and can perform a variety of functions, including providing an HTTP endpoint for serving non-.NET languages. We then built our worker role, which processes queued messages and updates our SQL Azure database.

12
Local Application for Updates

With our web service and worker roles in place, it's time to develop the application our drivers will use in order to confirm that the customer has accepted his/her vehicle. What we're about to do can be accomplished by any technology capable of calling a web service, but we'll use a simple Windows application to build on our strengths in .NET development. Our aim here is to cover some basics of Windows forms development, and one way to connect Windows Forms to Azure. However, there are entire books dedicated to Windows Forms Development, so we'll cover only a few things, including building a simple form to consume our web service in our web role, taking the returned data, and updating list boxes and a label.

Brief overview of the application

Our application has two purposes. The first purpose is to show the current status of an order. This is handled by selecting an order from the listbox and clicking a link to update a label with the selected order's status. This is done using our WCF web services by passing the OrderHeaderID to the web service and accepting the order status produced as output. The application will then update the label with the returned string.

The second purpose is to be able to update status for an order by selecting the order from the listbox, selecting the new order status for the order, and clicking a button to update the order. When the button is clicked, the OrderHeaderID for the selected order and the OrderStatusID for the selected status is sent via the web service and added to the queue for processing by our worker role.

How do our listboxes get populated? This is the third piece of our puzzle, and the answer to this, as you must have guessed based on previous chapters, is using our WCF service to retrieve the data for these. The data is requested at Form Load and bound to the listboxes immediately once it is returned from the web service.

JupiterMotorsERP local application

Adding our local application to the solution is very simple. Right-click on our solution, and choose **Add | New Project...**.

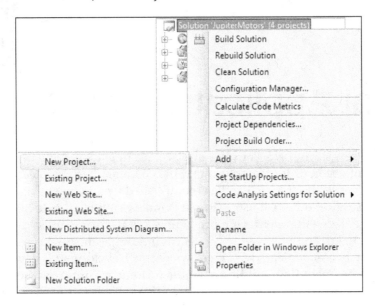

Under the project type **Windows**, select **Windows Forms Application**. Name the project as JupiterMotorsERP and click **OK**.

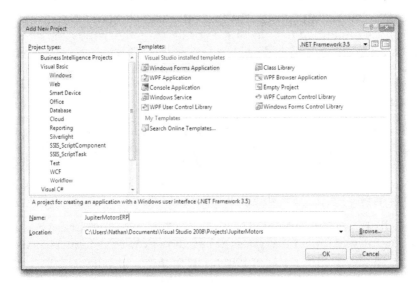

This will create a `Form1.vb` file and an `app.config` file. The `Form1.vb` will be our form design and code, whereas the `app.config` will hold any settings we wound need for the application.

As the first step toward setting up our local application, we're going to build the design of our form. We need the following:

- Two listboxes named `lbOrdersNotComplete` and `lbOrderStatuses`
- A label named `lCurrentStatus` and another named `lMessage`
- A link button called `lnkUpdateCurrentStatus`
- A button called `btnUpdateOrderStatus`

Our sample application form now looks like the following screenshot:

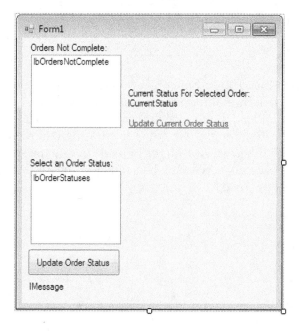

It's going to be a little tough for us to code our Windows Forms application to use our web services, as we haven't yet told the project where we're going to call the services. This is done by right-clicking on the project and choosing **Add Service Reference...**.

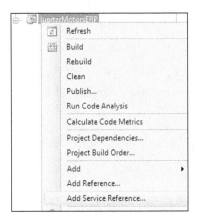

This is where Visual Studio does some great things. We can click the **Discover** button, and it will search the solution for available web services; we can also manually type in the URL of the service that we want to integrate with. For developing our application now, we're going to click the **Discover** button and let it find our web service in our WCF web role. Finally, name the service reference as `ERPServiceReference` and click **OK**. This will add the necessary code to `app.config`. We are now ready to run the application!

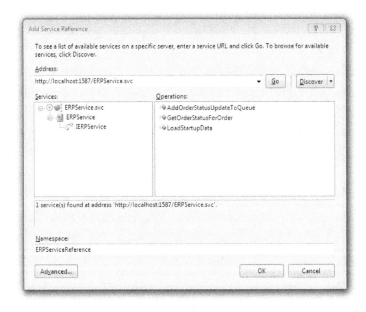

Adding App.config code

This code was inserted into the app.config file once the service reference was set up. We are good with using the code generated for us, but should any changes need to be made to the service reference (such as changing the endpoint from a local address to a production address), this is where you would make them:

```xml
<system.serviceModel>
    <bindings>
        <wsHttpBinding>
            <binding name="WSHttpBinding_IERPService"
             closeTimeout="00:01:00"
                openTimeout="00:01:00" receiveTimeout="00:10:00"
                  sendTimeout="00:01:00"
                bypassProxyOnLocal="false" transactionFlow="false"
                  hostNameComparisonMode="StrongWildcard"
                maxBufferPoolSize="524288"
                  maxReceivedMessageSize="65536"
                messageEncoding="Text" textEncoding="utf-8"
                  useDefaultWebProxy="true"
                allowCookies="false">
                <readerQuotas maxDepth="32"
                 maxStringContentLength="8192"
                    maxArrayLength="16384"
                    maxBytesPerRead="4096"
                    maxNameTableCharCount="16384" />
                <reliableSession ordered="true"
                 inactivityTimeout="00:10:00"
                    enabled="false" />
                <security mode="Message">
                    <transport clientCredentialType="Windows"
                     proxyCredentialType="None"
                        realm="">
                        <extendedProtectionPolicy
                         policyEnforcement="Never" />
                    </transport>
                    <message clientCredentialType="Windows"
                     negotiateServiceCredential="true"
                        algorithmSuite="Default" establishSecurity
                            Context="true" />
                </security>
            </binding>
        </wsHttpBinding>
    </bindings>
    <client>
        <endpoint address="http://localhost:1587/ERPService.svc"
         binding="wsHttpBinding"
```

```
                bindingConfiguration="WSHttpBinding_IERPService"
                  contract="ERPServiceReference.IERPService"
                name="WSHttpBinding_IERPService">
                <identity>
                    <dns value="localhost" />
                </identity>
            </endpoint>
        </client>
</system.serviceModel>
```

Now, if we double-click somewhere in the form, it will open up the code for our application. This is where we will add the following code to handle the web service calls, listbox, data bindings, and the events for the link and button clicks.

```
Public Class Form1
    Private Sub Form1_Load(ByVal sender As System.Object, ByVal e
       As System.EventArgs) Handles MyBase.Load
       Try
            Dim _client As New ERPServiceReference.ERPServiceClient
            Dim _resultsSet As New DataSet

            _resultsSet = _client.LoadStartupData()

            lbOrdersNotComplete.SelectedItem() = Nothing
            lbOrdersNotComplete.DataSource = _resultsSet.
               Tables("OrdersNotComplete").DefaultView
            lbOrdersNotComplete.DisplayMember = "CustomerPO"
            lbOrdersNotComplete.ValueMember = "OrderHeaderID"
            lbOrdersNotComplete.SelectedItem() = Nothing

            lbOrderStatuses.DataSource = _resultsSet.
               Tables("OrderStatuses").DefaultView
            lbOrderStatuses.DisplayMember = "Description"
            lbOrderStatuses.ValueMember = "OrderStatusID"
            lbOrderStatuses.SelectedItem() = Nothing

        Catch ex As Exception
            lMessage.Text = ex.Message()
        End Try
    End Sub

    Private Sub btnUpdateOrderStatus_Click(ByVal sender As
       System.Object, ByVal e As System.EventArgs)
       Handles btnUpdateOrderStatus.Click
```

```
        Dim _client As New ERPServiceReference.ERPServiceClient

        _client.AddOrderStatusUpdateToQueue(lbOrdersNotComplete.
            SelectedValue, lbOrderStatuses.SelectedValue)
    End Sub

    Private Sub lnkUpdateCurrentStatus_LinkClicked(ByVal
    sender As System.Object, ByVal e As System.Windows.Forms.
    LinkLabelLinkClickedEventArgs) Handles lnkUpdateCurrentStatus.
    LinkClicked
        Dim _client As New ERPServiceReference.ERPServiceClient

        lCurrentStatus.Text = _client.GetOrderStatusForOrder(
            lbOrdersNotComplete.SelectedValue)

    End Sub
End Class
```

Testing our application

To test our application, we need to run the entire solution in debug mode. We can easily do this in Visual Studio by pressing the *F5* button. The web role, worker role, and WCF web role should all start up in the development fabric once the solution is built, except our local application. Once all the web and worker roles have started, we can start an instance of our local application by right-clicking on the project and selecting **Debug | Start new instance**.

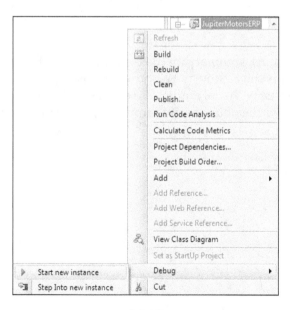

Our application will start up, bind the listboxes using the data returned from the web services, and allow us to now check the order statuses for any order not yet complete in the database. We can also change the status of any of these orders in the listbox. Note that the order status changes do not occur immediately. The changes are placed in the queue for processing and our worker role has a sleep timer on it. Once the worker role picks up the message, it is updated and can be checked by clicking the link and updating the label.

Summary

This chapter gave a quick summary on the concept behind the local application, some basic information on creating a Windows Forms application, and integrating it with web services using Visual Studio. We also used the web services to pull data into the application for data binding, and updating labels based on current data in the portal database.

13
Azure AppFabric

At the beginning of this book, we mentioned Microsoft's confusing product names, and AppFabric products are perhaps one of the most confusing. Azure AppFabric is one of two distinct Microsoft products that have the name AppFabric. The Azure AppFabric and the Windows Server AppFabric are not related to one another, and only the Azure AppFabric is part of the Azure platform. Now that we know which AppFabric we will be dealing with, let's see what it's all about. In this chapter, we'll cover:

- What Azure AppFabric is
- Overview of Access Control
- Configuring Access Control for Jupiter Motors
- Overview of Service Bus, including message relay and connection broker

Introduction to Azure AppFabric

Formerly known as .NET Services, Azure AppFabric provides both Access Control and Service Bus services. Access Control is a service where we can integrate third-party login services with our applications. Access Control can be used separately from the rest of Azure, so we can integrate Access Control with either our Azure applications or on premise applications.

The Service Bus service operates somewhat like a dynamic DNS service. If our partner's application needs to connect with us to transfer information (perhaps via FTP or AS2), we'd usually provide the partner with a static endpoint. A static endpoint is troublesome from a disaster recovery or maintenance window standpoint. Instead, we register our application in the Service Bus, and partner applications can communicate indirectly with us through the Service Bus, or the Service Bus can facilitate a direct connection. If publishing a public endpoint is not desirable, using the Service Bus can be a palatable alternative.

For greater detail and more examples on Azure AppFabric, Microsoft provides sample code, whitepapers, and webcasts on the AppFabric site at `http://msdn.microsoft.com/en-us/azure/netservices.aspx`. New features are being added to Azure AppFabric, and these features can be previewed at `https://portal.appfabriclabs.com/`.

Before any configuration can be performed, the Windows Azure AppFabric SDK needs to be downloaded and installed from `http://go.microsoft.com/fwlink/?LinkID=129448`. There are several files we need, the most important being the SDK and the samples, as each contains an Access Control configuration utility.

Access Control

Federated authentication is neither a new or unique concept. For instance, users of TweetPhoto do not need to create a separate account to log in—we can instead use our account from one of several popular social sites to log in at TweetPhoto, even though they are all separate and distinct companies.

When the **Sign in with Twitter** button is clicked, we're transferred to Twitter, and the URL contains an authentication token in the querystring. We'll look more at the OAuth protocol and these tokens later in this chapter, but sufficient to say for now, Twitter is the identity provider of the Twitterverse.

As an additional confirmation step, Twitter requires confirmation for the partner site to access a user's account, as seen in the following screenshot. This is a very good idea when there is user interaction, but for unattended systems this won't be possible. Fortunately, Access Control can be preconfigured to provide access using shared keys.

As the logins of these services are joined together, they are said to be **federated**. We see federation all over the Internet, where a single OpenId, Google, Twitter, Facebook, or Windows Live login can be used to access dozens or more additional services, or a single site can support logins from multiple other sites. The sites where we create an account are called **identity providers**, as our identity information is stored and provided by these services. Knowing that each identity provider is queried and returns data differently, we can appreciate the amount of work it would take to implement a number of popular sites, as well as add new identity providers and maintain any changes with currently supported providers.

One distinct difference between the Twitter example and Access Control is that a single Twitter account can be used on multiple websites, while Access Control is designed to integrate multiple identity providers into a single application.

If we don't actually log in to Access Control, what is it used for? Access Control is a **security token service** (STS) — a trusted application that issues security tokens via a standard interface. A security token is a small piece of text that contains identifying information and an encrypted signature that is used to assure the contents of the token.

So how do identity providers and Access Control fit together? Every identity provider returns identity data in a different format, which our application would need to parse correctly. That could mean a lot of work and rework as APIs change or are added. As application developers, we use Access Control to configure which identity providers we trust, and remap the properties from each into a single format our application can consume. The goal of Access Control is to federate identity providers into a single common format that our application can understand. If we're developing a very private application, Access Control may not be all that interesting, and there are other means we could use (such as the standard ASP.NET login provider). However, if we're developing a public application (like a forum site), this is a very exciting service. As new providers emerge or current ones change their API, we do not need to make any changes to our application code; we only need to make configuration changes in Access Control so that our application can integrate with the latest popular Internet sites.

The little pieces of information about a user such as the username, first name, last name, and so on are called "claims". An identity is the full set of claims that represents a user. When a user accesses a site and logs in, the user ID is a claim being made by that user. By claim we mean when a user enters his/her ID while logging in to a site, he/she is trying to say that "I am this identity on this site." The verification for that claim is entering the correct password.

These days, on a majority of sites, we must create a unique account for each one, and each site then stores our identity separately as compared to other sites. By contrast, Access Control does not store any identity information. Our service trusts the information from the identity provider because we told Access Control to trust the claims from the provider, and our application trusts Access Control.

Because Access Control is RESTful, Access Control can be utilized by any application, and on any platform that can consume REST data. It's important to note that Access Control can be the only Azure service we use, and the application that consumes Access Control tokens can be written in any language.

> Even though we just said that we don't log in to Access Control, Access Control does support simple symmetric key logins, which can be used as a rudimentary user ID/password system; however, it is not the main purpose behind Access Control and its capability for authentication services is very limited.
>
> For additional information on Access Control, see Channel 9's Identity and the Windows Azure Platform Training Course at `http:// channel9.msdn.com/learn/courses/Azure/IdentityAzure/`.

Authentication versus authorization

We've mentioned the terms authentication and authorization, and it's worth discussing the difference between the two. In a claims-based identity model like Access Control, authentication and authorization are separated from each other and the rest of the application code.

Authentication establishes the identity of the user. This can be as simple as a username/password, or as secure as a retina scan. Once the user is authenticated, our application can determine what actions the user is then authorized to perform.

In Access Control, we do not configure authentication; we configure trust relationships with the identity providers. We do configure authorization rules (discussed further), which our application consumes and respects.

Basics of Access Control configuration

When it comes to configuring Access Control, there is some good news and some bad news. First, the good news: one day, Access Control may be a very useful service for a considerable number of applications, whether or not these applications are hosted on Azure. Now the bad news: at the time of writing, only symmetric key and Active Directory Federation Services 2.0 (ADFS) are supported. The long-term goal is to support every major identity provider, but we're not there yet. At the rate Microsoft is developing Azure, it may not be too far, but no promises have been made.

More good news: all configuration changes can be accomplished through a REST interface. More bad news: at the time of writing, there were no online tools; all configuration changes are handled through local tools that wrap the REST requests. One tool is a command line in the SDK called ACM.EXE, the other is a sample called ACMBROWSER. A very good overview of configuring Access Control using ACM is found in the whitepaper at `http://go.microsoft.com/fwlink/?LinkID=150096`, and a simple tutorial is found at `http://msdn.microsoft.com/en-us/library/ee706752%28v=MSDN.10%29.aspx`.

The lowest level of configuration in Access Control is a rule. Each rule specifies something about a supported identity provider, such as the name, ID, algorithm, key, or which actions users from this provider can perform. Rules are not configured or used separately, but are done so as part of a RuleSet. Alongside a RuleSet, we also configure a **Token Policy**, which sets the timeout for security token issued by Access Control. Together, the RuleSet and Token Policy form the Scope. A service (such as a web role) can have multiple scopes, and the scopes associated with a service are collectively known as the **Service Policy**. A Service Policy is applied to a Service Namespace, which organizes the rules for a resource and segregates transactions on the billing statement (allowing us to use one AppFabric account for many applications).

Currently, only one RuleSet is allowed per scope, but each service can have multiple scopes. Also, at the time of writing, a RuleSet cannot be shared across different scopes—even if they contain the same information, the RuleSet must be created for each scope.

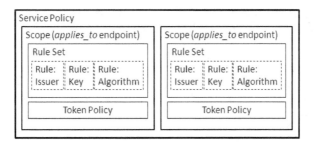

Requests and Simple Web Tokens

The point of this configuration is to be able to retrieve access tokens from Access Control, so it's necessary to discuss the tokens themselves. Access Control returns a type of token called a **Simple Web Token (SWT)**. SWT is a recent token specification developed by a group of Internet leaders, including Microsoft and Google. SWT was developed to be structurally and cryptographically simple, and to be compact. The small size of an SWT means it can be easily transmitted in HTTP headers or as part of a querystring.

SWTs are a type of access token that are utilized in Web Resource Authentication Protocol (WRAP), which is itself an extension of OAuth called OAuth-WRAP, and the upcoming OAuth 2.0 specification.

For a little history, OAuth was developed in part by some of the developers of OpenID. OpenID works great for an individual to log in to many websites with a single credential; however, with the rise of web services and APIs, a better system was needed. OAuth was designed to allow third-party applications to access secured resources (such as TweetPhoto being able to post a new photo upload on the user's Twitter account). OAuth was comprehensive, but also complicated to implement. OAuth-WRAP is a subsequent implementation of OAuth, and served to rectify some of the complaints about OAuth. On the other hand, OAuth 2.0 is an upcoming upgrade to OAuth intended to simplify the protocol further. The specs and ongoing discussion of WRAP and SWT can be found at `http://groups.google.com/group/oauth-wrap-wg`.

Requests can be made for either a plaintext token or a **simple web token (SWT)**. All token requests sent to Access Control are made using HTTPS protocol and form POST method. Request data are form-encoded, and the scope parameter (named `wrap_scope` in the request) URL-encoded as well. SWTs are signed with an HMACSHA256 signature.

The SWTs returned from Access Control are URL-encoded and are part of a longer return string. To use them, we must parse them from the return string and decode them. Additionally, we should ensure the token is valid before allowing the user to access any secured resources. Validations should include confirming the signature is a valid HMACSHA256 signature, whether or not the token has expired, and that the issuer and audience values match what was requested.

A raw token has the following format:

```
Issuer=https://<serviceNamespace>.accesscontrol.windows.net/WRAPv0.9/
&Audience=<requested appliesto>
&<claim type1>=<claim value1>,<claim value2>...<claim valueN>
&ExpiresOn=<expires date>
&HMACSHA256=<hmac signature>
```

Essentially, a token is just a series of name/value pairs. The HMAC256 signature should always be the last name/value in the token.

Additional documentation about tokens and requests can be found at `http://msdn.microsoft.com/en-us/library/ee706734.aspx`.

Configuring Access Control for Jupiter Motors

It's now time to configure Access Control for the Jupiter Motors client application. The first thing we need to do is plan who we want to access our web service, and what actions can be performed. For this web service offered by Jupiter Motors, it's pretty simple—only our client application should have access, and it can call any of the three functions in the service. Just as a reminder, the functions are:

- `LoadStartupData`: The function returns two datasets, one containing the possible statuses for an order and the other containing the orders waiting completion

- `GetStatusForOrder`: This function returns the status of a selected order

- `AddOrderStatusUpdateToQueue`: This function puts the status update into a queue to be processed by our worker role

We need to create a ruleset allowing access to these functions, as well as the token policies and scopes. As we're providing access to internally developed applications, we can use the simple symmetric key functionality, similar to a user ID and password. Additionally, we need to enable an SSL on our portal to secure the data being transferred.

Configuring Azure AppFabric Portal

Before any requests can be made of Azure AppFabric, we need to obtain the Management Key. This key is included in the corresponding request to prove we are able to make the request by having secret information. This key should be protected carefully. To find the Management Key, we need to log in to the Azure AppFabric portal at `http://appfabric.azure.com/`. After we've logged in, we can see details of our project and the Service Namespaces, if there are any, as shown in the following screenshot:

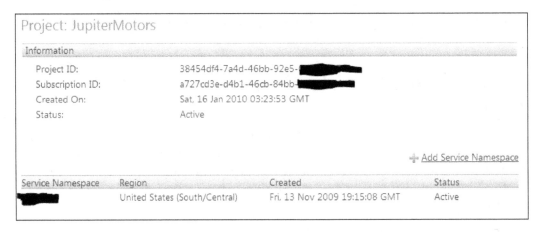

As we have an existing Service Namespace, we can click on its name to be taken to the Service Namespace details page. The top section, named **Manage**, contains both the **Current Management Key** and **Previous Management Key**. Both keys are supported in case any key is changed before all existing applications are updated.

If there is no Service Namespace listed, or if we need to create a new Service Namespace, there is a link on the project summary page (shown in the screenshot prior to the preceding one) that we use to create a new Service Namespace. To create a Service Namespace, we follow these steps:

1. The first step in creating a new Service Namespace is to choose the name we want to use to refer to the namespace. As the name we choose must be unique across all of Azure, it's important to validate it.

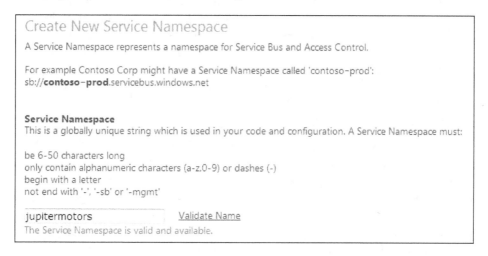

2. The next step is to choose the region in which our Service Namespace is to be run. At the time of writing, there were only four regions to choose from. These regions do not refer to a particular data center, but to a geographic region in which one or more data centers are located.

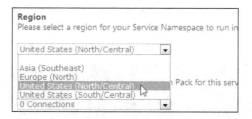

3. Finally, if we're planning to use the Service Bus, we can choose the number of connections. We'll discuss more about this in the further sections, but we will configure the connections at the same time.

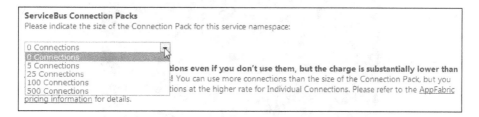

Configuration tools

At the time of writing, there is no way to configure Access Control via the portal. All configuration steps must be performed using REST calls to the configuration service from client tools. Fortunately, the Windows Azure AppFabric SDK (download from `http://go.microsoft.com/fwlink/?LinkID=129448`) includes a tool called ACM.exe that is used to configure Access Control. A full reference for ACM.EXE can be found at `http://msdn.microsoft.com/en-us/library/ee706706.aspx`. The C# source code is also included in case we need a reference, or we want to develop our own configuration tool.

An additional tool called AcmBrowser is provided in the AppFabric samples. The samples can be downloaded from `http://go.microsoft.com/fwlink/?LinkID=129448` and installed separately from the SDK. AcmBrowser is a GUI tool that can be used to configure Access Control, and display the configuration in a more user-friendly manner than Acm.exe. The AcmBrowser project is located at `<installfolder>\AccessControl\ExploringFeatures\Management\AcmBrowser\ManagementBrowser`. In order to use AcmBrowser, we have to open the project and compile the tool. At the time of writing, Acm.exe is the recommended tool to use, and it provides useful output, so we'll use it ourselves.

The acm.exe syntax is standard verb-noun:

```
acm.exe <command> <resource> [-option:<option value>]
```

If the only option is "-?", help for that command/resource will be returned. For example, `Tools>acm.exe -?` returns the following help information:

More detailed help is also available for individual commands:

For a complete overview of the commands, resources, and options, the MSDN documentation is available at `http://msdn.microsoft.com/en-us/library/ee706706.aspx`. Some of the options we need to include with every operation toward Access Control are the Host, the Service Namespace, and the Management Key. Looking once again at the management key shown above, we surely don't want to have to type that too many times! Fortunately, we can add these three values to the config files and omit them from the command line.

The `Acm.exe` and `acm.exe.config` files are installed by default at `C:\Program Files\Windows Azure platform AppFabric SDK\V1.0\Tools`. We can edit the config file to provide the three options. The host is defaulted to the management web service address, `accesscontrol.windows.net`, and should not be changed. We can copy and paste the values for the Service Namespace and Management Key from the Azure AppFabric portal, creating the file shown here:

```xml
<?xml version="1.0" encoding="utf-8" ?>
<configuration>
  <appSettings>
    <add key="host" value="accesscontrol.windows.net"/>
    <add key="service" value="jupiter"/>
    <add key="mgmtkey" value="xr5BwkhSynQ+RwGbxGEkDUepB+zrF9p8qimhfqm
CPZ0="/>
  </appSettings>
</configuration>
```

At this point in the configuration process, we have a Service Namespace that does not yet have a Service Policy.

Referring to the diagram under the *Basics of Access Control configuration* section, we can see that we have Rule Sets, Token Policies, and Scopes to configure to create a Service Policy.

Two of the most useful commands in Acm.exe are get and getall. We use get to retrieve information on a particular Scope/Token Policy/Rule/Issuer, and we use the getall command to retrieve a list of all the Scopes/Token Policies/Rules/Issuers. The ID of the object is needed for the get command. So, as we add objects to Access Control, it's a good idea to record the details.

To confirm we don't have a scope in our Service Policy, we can use the getall command:

```
Tools>acm.exe getall scope
```

The count of the scopes in our Service Policy will be shown in the output:

```
        Count: 0
```

The count of 0 confirms we do not have any scopes. We can repeat the process for Rules, Token Policies, and Issuers.

Creating a Token Policy

A Token Policy dictates the lifetime of a token (to help prevent it from being reused) and whether to autogenerate a signing key or use a static key. The command to create a Token Policy is:

```
acm.exe create tokenpolicy
```

By adding the "-?" option, we can list all options available for this command, as shown here:

Recall that the Service, Host, and Management Key are already set in the configuration file. All we need to do to create a Token Policy is to set the name and key value:

```
Tools>acm.exe create tokenpolicy -name:Delivery -autogeneratekey
```

If our Token Policy is created successfully, the ID of the policy will be returned.

```
Object created successfully (ID:' tp_4ef493f23daf444ca50410a7d1852125')
```

When using the autogeneratekey option, the timeout is defaulted to 8 hours. If we were using a static key, we'd specify the key value in the command (type carefully!). For applications used in public environments, we would probably want to set the timeout to a shorter value. Note that the ID begins with `tp_`. This differentiates the Token Policy IDs from other Access Control IDs.

It's a good idea to store the information for each object we create in a password keeper or database for future reference. We'll need the IDs for the next configuration steps and in some of our applications.

If we need to retrieve the details of our Token Policy, we can again use the `getall` command to retrieve the details of all Token Policies:

```
Tools>acm.exe getall tokenpolicy
```

We can see the ID of our Token Policy, as well as the friendly name, the timeout, and the signing key issued to our request:

```
        Count: 1


           id: tp_4ef493f23daf444ca50410a7d1852125
         name: Delivery
      timeout: 28800
          key: 14K+qOU9OTo1dG3DWxluH+eTvsX/CBHhFbxLfxZcjC4=
```

Let's see how the `get` command works, specifying the ID as part of the options:

```
Tools>acm.exe get tokenpolicy
-id:tp_4ef493f23daf444ca50410a7d1852125
```

The following information is returned:

```
           id: tp_4ef493f23daf444ca50410a7d1852125
         name: Delivery
      timeout: 28800
          key: 14K+qOU9OTo1dG3DWxluH+eTvsX/CBHhFbxLfxZcjC4=
```

The information returned is the same as with the `getall` command. So far, so good — now we need to create a scope, an issuer, and a rule.

Configuring a Scope

A scope groups the rules and token policies as they relate to a specific URI. In order to create a scope, we need to include the Token Policy ID we want associated with it.

```
Tools>acm.exe create scope -name:DeliveryScope
-appliesto:http://jupitermotors.com/deliveryservice
-tokenpolicyid:tp_4ef493f23daf444ca50410a7d1852125
```

If our scope creation is successful, the ID of the scope is returned.

```
Object created successfully (ID:'scp_334a7c77845e7ac20764300da9119c434ffc
c65d')
```

The IDs for scopes begin with `scp_`, just as the IDs for token policies began with `tp_`. We now have a scope, tied to a URI and with a token policy. We need this ID to create a rule, so it's a good idea to copy and paste this ID. It's now time to create an issuer and a rule.

Configuring an Issuer

An **Issuer** is another name for an Identity Provider. Users create accounts with Identity Providers, and Identity Providers issue claims to consuming services. In the current scenario, Access Control is the identity consumer. We establish a trust between Access Control and the Issuer with a secret key provided by the Issuer. The ultimate claims consumer — our local application — isn't concerned with anything other than a trust relationship with Access Control.

```
Tools>acm.exe create issuer -name:jupiter -issuername:jupiter -
autogeneratekey
Object created successfully (ID:'iss_
a2f7fcb5afeb7983ffbb6ce3d1a7e91edf321350')
```

If our issuer is created successfully, the ID is returned. As with all the other IDs we've created, Issuer IDs begin with a distinct prefix. We'll use this ID to create a rule allowing access to applications presenting the correct key, so be sure to copy and paste it, too.

Configuring a Rule

Rules are where the magic happens. We'll use Rules to map claims, and we use rules to configure trusts with Issuers. The mapping is done with the `inclaimtype`, `inclaimvalue`, `outclaimtype`, and `outclaimvalue` options.

When we create a Rule, we need to include a Scope ID and an Issuer ID. Because the IDs are long, it might be easiest to build the command in a text editor first, and then copy the command to the command window.

```
Tools>acm.exe create rule -name:jupiterrule1 -scopeid:scp_
334a7c77845e7ac2076430
```

```
0da9119c434ffcc65d -inclaimissuerid:iss_
a2f7fcb5afeb7983ffbb6ce3d1a7e91edf321350
```

```
 -inclaimtype:Issuer -inclaimvalue:jupiter -outclaimtype:role -
outclaimvalue:user
```

On success, the rule ID is returned, which begins with `rul_`.

```
Object created successfully (ID:'rul_
42db52d7749770ca2f585ddc1b992adecb8b76bf93f
```

```
b4ba4e250ab8acfd387b647ff644ffafcb5f4')
```

We have now created a rule that says anyone who presents a valid key from the "jupiter" issuer is placed in the user role. As we add additional identity providers to our service policy, we need to perform only these four configuration steps to map visitors into the "users" role.

Configuring a client application for Access Control

When a service is secured by Access Control, a client does not make its first request directly to the service. Instead, we need to perform the following steps:

1. Request a token from Access Control.
2. Split the token out of the response from Access Control.
3. Build the service request, including the necessary parameters and the token.
4. Issue the service request.
5. Receive and process the response from the service.

A client can cache the token and use it until the token expires. Once a token expires, the client application must request a new token before it can make any additional requests from the service.

In order to request a token from Access Control, we need to know the Service Namespace, the scope, and the issuer key. Because these values may change (especially the issuer key), it's advisable to place them in the application settings or our client application:

Name	Type		Scope		Value
IssuerKey	String	▾	Application	▾	iss_a2f7fcb5afeb7983ffbb6ce3d1a7e91edf321350
ServiceNamespace	String	▾	Application	▾	jupiter
Scope	String	▾	Application	▾	http://jupitermotors.cloudapp.net/

Requesting the Token

The first modification to our code is we need to add two `Imports` statements:

```
Imports System.Net
Imports System.Collections.Specialized
```

We now create a `POST` request to Access Control, and pass the IssuerKey and Scope settings we defined earlier. The response is returned as a byte array, which we then convert to a UTF8 encoded string:

```
Dim _client As New WebClient()
_client.BaseAddress = String.Format("https://{0}.accesscontrol.
windows.net/", My.Settings.ServiceNamespace)

Dim _values As New NameValueCollection()
_values.Add("wrap_name", "wcfauthmanager")
_values.Add("wrap_password", My.Settings.IssuerKey)
_values.Add("wrap_scope", My.Settings.Scope)

Dim _responseBytes() As Byte = _client.UploadValues("WRAPv0.9/",
"POST", _values)

Dim _response As String = System.Text.Encoding.UTF8.GetString(_
responseBytes)
```

At this point, we now have our token, but it's part of a much larger string. We have to unpack the token by splitting apart the name/value pairs with the name `wrap_access_token=`, and taking the value:

```
Dim _pairs() As String = _response.Split("&"c)

Dim _tokenPair As String = From p In _pairs Select p Where
p.Contains("wrap_access_token=")

Dim _token As String = _tokenPair.Split("="c)(1)
```

Now we're ready to make requests from our web service. This will require some changes to previously written and tested code. If our client project doesn't have references for System.ServiceModel and System.ServiceModel.Web, these need to be added. We also need to add an Imports System.ServiceModel to our form.

As we need to modify the request headers to include the token, we'll need to create a request proxy, add the token (remember we need to UrlDecode the token) as the "authorization" header, and then call the service.

```vb
Private Function LoadFormStartupData(ByVal _token As String) As
DataSet

Dim _startup As DataSet

Dim _binding As New WebHttpBinding(WebHttpSecurityMode.None)
Dim _address As New Uri(My.Settings.Scope)

Dim _channelFactory As New WebChannelFactory(Of ERPServiceReference.
IERPServiceChannel)(_binding, _address)

Dim _proxy As ERPServiceReference.IERPServiceChannel = _
channelFactory.CreateChannel()

Using TempOperationContextScope As OperationContextScope = New Operati
onContextScope(TryCast(_proxy, IContextChannel))

Dim authHeaderValue As String = String.Format("WRAP access_
token=""{0}""", System.Web.HttpUtility.UrlDecode(_token))

WebOperationContext.Current.OutgoingRequest.Headers.
Add("authorization", authHeaderValue)

_startup = _proxy.LoadStartupData

End Using

CType(_proxy, IClientChannel).Close()
_channelFactory.Close()

Return _startup
End Function
```

Using Access Control in a web service

We're now set to add Access Control to our web service. We have a couple of configuration values we need, and a config file is the ideal place, in case we need to edit these values later. The usual place is in a `web.config` file, but recall that the `web.config` files are deployed as part of the compiled binary on Azure. Instead, we need to use the `csconfig` file. The two settings we need to add are the Token Policy ID and the Service Namespace. We use these as our known values when we compare the tokens presented by the client application.

To add our settings to the WCF Role's `csconfig` file, right-click the `JupiterMotorsWCFRole`, listed under the `Roles` folder, and select **Properties**.

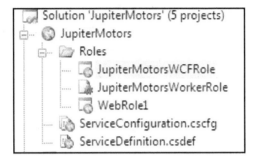

On the **Settings** tab, add our two settings.

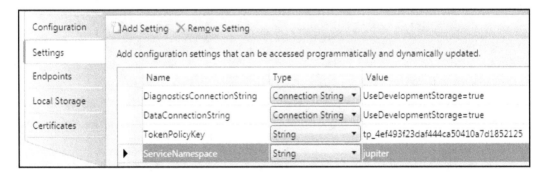

Before we accept any tokens presented to us, we need to validate them. We can write our own token validation, but the AppFabric SDK includes a couple of classes we can use as a starting point. The `WCFAuthorizationManager` project (found in `<%install_path%>\Access Control\Exploring Features`) contains an `ACSAuthorizationManager` class and a `TokenValidator` class we can use. `ACSAuthorizationManager` is an implementation of `ServiceAuthorizationManager`, and performs the following verifications of a request:

- It checks whether there is an authorization entry in the request headers. If not, the request is rejected.

- If there is an authorization token in the request headers, call the `TokenValidator.Validate` method. If the token is not valid, the request is rejected.

- Claims are extracted from the token, including a claim of type "action". We then determine what action the user is attempting to perform (or what method is being called). If there is no action, the request is rejected.

- If all checks out, the action is allowed.

The `TokenValidator` class performs the following verifications of the token:

- Confirms the HMAC signature is valid

- Confirms the token has not expired

- Confirms the issuer is trusted

- Confirms the audience is trusted

We should add these two files to the `JupiterMotorsWCFRole` project. We may need to add a missing reference to `System.ServiceModel.Web` in order for the project to compile.

Service Bus

If you hear "Service Bus" and think of the Enterprise Service Bus (ESB) pattern, you're on to something. The name is no accident—the Azure Service Bus is designed to be an implementation of the ESB pattern.

If you're not familiar with the **ESB**, then for this discussion you need to know it's a systems architecture that connects any number of enterprise applications through a single intermediate, known as the "bus". The bus brokers messages between systems and handles authentication, among other functions. The software found in an ESB implementation is often known as "middleware". The typical ESB pattern is used to connect applications within the same enterprise.

The Service Bus handles similar functions as an ESB, but between applications in different enterprises. The Service Bus can securely relay messages from other enterprises to and from WCF endpoints hosted behind our firewall. In this relay mode, we do not need to open ports or reconfigure our firewall. The Service Bus can also facilitate direct connections between applications in two enterprises.

Our current portal design doesn't include a need for the Service Bus, but it's a feature we want to keep our eyes on for future use (one of our portal project managers mentioned there was some talk of integrating third-party dealership applications), so we'll discuss it here as we're working in the AppFabric. The official MSDN documentation for the Service Bus is located at `http://msdn.microsoft.com/en-us/library/ee732537.aspx`. For an additional reference, Channel 9 has made available a Windows Azure Service Bus Training Course documentation at `http://channel9.msdn.com/learn/courses/Azure/ServiceBus/`.

Service Bus as message relay

If we're going to integrate a third-party dealership application, we need a way to exchange messages with it from our ERP system. Customers want to know the available options, price, and time to delivery, and orders need to be placed automatically, so there may be several messages exchanged between systems. Compounding the work is the need to support many third-party systems used by a large number of dealers, all the while keeping our internal network secure.

To integrate with a number of third-party applications, web services are the way to go. However, we don't want to open our system to the world, and we don't want to be forced into implementing special configurations (such as router whitelists) for every dealer. This is where Service Bus is of great help.

One of the functions of Service Bus is as a message relay. We would only need to connect our systems with Service Bus, and use the Service Bus as our public endpoint. Clients make requests to Service Bus and, if the requests authenticate properly, the requests are relayed to our systems. Our responses are sent to the Service Bus, and are then relayed back to the clients. Messages are relayed between our systems and the Service Bus via a persistent two-way connection.

This approach has a number of advantages:

- As the connection between our applications and the Service Bus originates from our systems, and is a two-way connection, there is no need for NAT rules or firewall exceptions.

- The Service Bus has a stable URL and a message buffer, in case our systems disconnect. Should our systems fail and we need to invoke our disaster recovery plan, messages to our system can be buffered, and retrieved once our system is online again. Our clients won't see any interruption.

- Our systems are shielded against attacks such as denial-of-service, as the actual service address would not be known. The DoS attack would be directed against Azure (which has the resources and security to deal with such attacks), rather than our internal systems.

There are also a couple of disadvantages to consider:

- We must pay for an additional service, which introduces some direct cost.

- Configuration is stored on a distant system, ultimately out of the control of our network administrators. Our network administrators may not like that idea.

- We'll need to make some changes in our programming to support persistent connections and other aspects of the Service Bus.

Service Bus as connection broker

If relaying messages isn't to our liking, there is a second option. Service Bus can broker direct connections between our system and the third-party system. The process starts with third-party systems making a request to Service Bus, which has an open connection from our system. The service bus then facilitates the two connections, finding a common protocol on which to communicate, and the two applications then use a direct connection. Either of these two scenarios may be of interest to us should the rumored third-party integration become reality.

Summary

In this chapter, we examined the Windows Azure AppFabric. The two services that comprise AppFabric are Access Control and Service Bus. Access Control issues signed web tokens (SWT) as part of a claims-based identity system, and can be used by applications hosted both on Azure and on premises. Access Control currently supports symmetric key and ADFS v2, and the stated long-term goal is to federate the major identity providers, greatly reducing the amount of time and work in order for our applications to support these identity providers. We then configured Access Control to be used by our delivery confirmation application.

We also examined the Service Bus, which facilitates communications between applications located in two different enterprises. The Service Bus can operate as a message relay or a connection broker, and these functions may be of interest to us in a future phase of our project.

14
Azure Monitoring and Diagnostics

When we host a site on our own servers, we have complete and direct access to the event logs, the IIS logs, and the performance counters. When something is amiss, these resources are our first stop for diagnostic information, and more often than not, the answer is found in these resources. Because we can't access an Azure instance in the same way as we connect via Remote Desktop to our on-premises server, how do we get the same information? Fortunately, Microsoft has provided mechanisms for us, and that's what we'll explore here (Microsoft has announced Remote Desktop access to Azure instances, as well as improved diagnostics, but those are not available at the time of writing). In this chapter, we'll cover the following topics:

- Examining what information can be collected via Azure diagnostics
- Learning how to enable collection of diagnostic data
- Implementing diagnostic data collection in our portal app
- Persisting collected data in the proper storage service

Azure Diagnostics—under the hood

When we consider working with Azure diagnostics, we need to decide what to collect and how to store the collected data. The following table summarizes the information available to us:

Data	Collected by default	Role(s)	Storage	Storage location name
Windows Azure logs	Yes	Web, Worker	Table	`WadLogsTable`
IIS logs	Yes	Web	Blob	`wad-iis-logfiles`
Windows diagnostic logs	Yes	Web, Worker	Table	`WadLogsTable`
Failed request logs	No	Web	Blob	`wad-iis-failedreqlogfiles`
Windows event logs	No	Web, Worker	Table	`WadWindowsEventLogsTable`
Performance counters	No	Web, Worker	Table	`WadPerformanceCountersTable`
Crash dumps	No	Web, Worker	Blob	`wad-crash-dumps`
Custom error logs	No	Web, Worker	Blob	user defined storage

On a traditional Windows system, IIS logs, crash dumps and failed request logs would be stored in files. These three logs are referred to as *Directory* logs in Azure's jargon, and end up in blobs. Except for custom logs, the rest of the logs are all persisted in tables.

During data collection, information is buffered in a blob, inside a container named `wad-control-container`. Diagnostic data are not accessible until they are transferred from `wad-control-container` to the proper blob or table storage. The diagnostic buffers can be manipulated via descendants of the `DiagnosticDataBufferConfiguration` class, an overview of which can be found at `http://nmackenzie.spaces.live.com/blog/cns!B863FF075995D18A!536.entry`.

There is also a much more sophisticated framework for logging and tracing, based in part on the **Event Tracing for Windows** (ETW) framework we may already be familiar with. Samples are available for downloading at `http://code.msdn.microsoft.com/WADiagnostics`. Microsoft also provides a number of additional samples in the Azure SDK and other sample downloads.

Diagnostic ETW data are available through classes in the `System.Diagnostics` namespace. Windows Azure Diagnostics extends this namespace with the `Microsoft.WindowsAzure.Diagnostics` namespace. References for the `Microsoft.WindowsAzure.Diagnostics` can be found at `http://msdn.microsoft.com/en-us/library/microsoft.windowsazure.diagnostics.aspx` and `http://msdn.microsoft.com/en-us/library/microsoft.windowsazure.diagnostics.management.aspx`. As a general outline, when we implement logging, the general process flow looks like the following diagram:

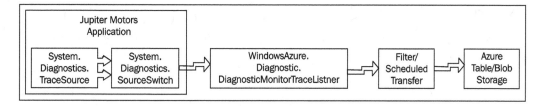

In the architecture depicted in this diagram, our application pipes diagnostic data through `TraceSources`, which are intermediate objects (of type `System.Diagnostics.TraceSource`) used to route data to various endpoints. A `SourceSwitch`, where we see values such as "verbose" or "critical", determines which messages should be passed to the `DiagnosticMonitorTraceListener`. On a normal system, verbose data could be routed through a `TraceSource` with a log file endpoint, while critical errors might be routed through a `TraceSource` that sends a text message to a sysadmin.

`TraceListeners` subscribe to `TraceSources`, and route the data to the desired endpoint. The default `TraceListener` in Azure is the `DiagnosticMonitor`, which is a special class used to configure the collection of diagnostic data. A diagnostic monitor can be configured to listen to a number of `TraceSources`. In Azure, diagnostic data are all routed to either Table or Blob Storage.

The three logs indicated as being part of the default Diagnostic Monitor collection— Azure, IIS 7, and Windows Diagnostic—are enabled by default when we use one of the Azure templates. Because our sample is using a default template, there is nothing much that we have to do. If we were to use our own template, we'd have to make sure we included the initialization (refer to `http://msdn.microsoft.com/en-us/library/ee843890.aspx`). The other logs can be collected, but additional coding is required to activate them.

Although we may activate log collection, that does not make the log data available to us immediately upon collection. We also need to transfer the log data to a store we can access, such as Table Storage. This must be done whether we're using the default Diagnostic Monitor or we've activated an additional log source.

The **Hello Fabric** sample in the Azure SDK is a useful reference for experimenting with diagnostic logging. It's a very simple application that can be run in the development fabric on a development machine.

Enabling diagnostic logging

When we create an Azure application using one of the default templates, collection of Windows Azure, IIS, and Windows Diagnostic logs is enabled by default. We can see the setup in the template files.

The `DiagnosticMonitorTraceListener` configuration for our WCF and web role projects is found in the `web.config` file:

```
<system.diagnostics>
  <trace>
    <listeners>
      <add type="Microsoft.WindowsAzure.Diagnostics.
DiagnosticMonitorTraceListener, Microsoft.WindowsAzure.Diagnostics,
Version=1.0.0.0, Culture=neutral, PublicKeyToken=31bf3856ad364e35"
name="AzureDiagnostics">
        <filter type=""/>
      </add>
    </listeners>
  </trace>
</system.diagnostics>
```

There are a number of additional configuration options in the `<system.diagnostics>` element; complete documentation can be found at `http://msdn.microsoft.com/en-us/library/1txedc80.aspx`. Specifically, the `<filter>` element (`http://msdn.microsoft.com/en-us/library/ms229326.aspx`) is used to set the `SourceSwitch` filtering values.

The `DiagnosticMonitorTraceListener` is started in our projects' `OnStart` method, found in the `webrole.vb` file:

```
Public Overrides Function OnStart() As Boolean

    DiagnosticMonitor.Start("DiagnosticsConnectionString")

    ...
End Function
```

In our `workerrole.vb` file, we have the following entry in the `Run` method that logs the start of the role.

```
Public Overrides Sub Run()

Trace.WriteLine("JupiterMotorsWorkerRole entry point called.",
"Information")

...

End Sub
```

If we weren't using a template, we'd need to add this code manually to the proper files to enable collection of diagnostic data.

Enabling the additional logging types is easy, but not all the logs are implemented in the same way. For instance, the Failed Request Logs are enabled by editing the `web.config` file, whereas the Windows Event Logs are enabled with some code in the `Role.OnStart` method. The MSDN documentation for enabling other sources of diagnostic information can be found at `http://msdn.microsoft.com/en-us/library/ee843890.aspx`.

One of the more interesting and useful sources of diagnostic information is performance counters. We've all probably used performance counters in the past when debugging all sorts of issues, and Azure provides us with the same capabilities. The downside to performance counters is that we configure them in the `Role.OnStart()` method, so we must redeploy our application if we want to change them. One possibility would be to preconfigure a number of performance counters, wrapped in `if...then` blocks that check for values in the config files. This way, we can turn collection of performance counters on and off by editing the proper config file. The following is the configuration for the % Processor Time counter. Note that there is a very specific format used for the `CounterSpecifier`. For additional information on this naming format, we can review the documentation at `http://msdn.microsoft.com/en-us/library/aa373193%28VS.85%29.aspx`.

```
Public Overrides Function OnStart() As Boolean

Dim diagConfig As DiagnosticMonitorConfiguration = DiagnosticMonitor.
GetDefaultInitialConfiguration()

Dim procTimeConfig As PerformanceCounterConfiguration = New
PerformanceCounterConfiguration()

procTimeConfig.CounterSpecifier = "\Processor(*)\% Processor Time"
```

```
procTimeConfig.SampleRate = System.TimeSpan.FromSeconds(1.0)

diagConfig.PerformanceCounters.DataSources.Add(procTimeConfig)

DiagnosticMonitor.Start("DiagnosticsConnectionString")

Return MyBase.OnStart()

End Function
```

A list of available performance counters can be found at
`http://technet.microsoft.com/en-us/library/cc774901(WS.10).aspx`.

Diagnostic configuration is not global—configuration applies only to the role where we have added the code. We need to be sure to configure data collection for each and every role we want to be able to debug (which is pretty much every role). If we're interested in the same information, it's just copy-and-paste code, but we still need to remember to do it.

Changing the location of the logging configuration

In an ASP.NET application, the usual place to configure `SourceSwitches` and other configuration details is in the `web.config` file. This way, if we need to change the level of diagnostic information collected, we can simply edit the `web.config` and commence debugging. By default, the diagnostic configuration information for an Azure application is stored in the `web.config` file. However, Azure applications are not deployed in the same way as ASP.NET applications. Azure applications are compiled into a single file and deployed as a single file. We cannot simply edit a `web.config` (or an `app.config` in the case of a worker role) once an Azure application is deployed. If we need to edit the `web.config` or `app.config`, we would need to edit the files locally and redeploy the entire application post-edit.

With Azure applications, the recommendation is to duplicate configuration settings into both the `web.config` and the `.cscfg` file. The `.cscfg` file can be changed while the application is running, but the `web.config` cannot be changed in the application. This setup requires a little extra effort at the beginning, but the effort can be worth it when needed. The idea behind duplicating the configuration is that an application can be deployed on Azure, and then later redeployed on premises without any additional modification. If this application is sure to not be deployed on IIS, the `web.config` edit can be skipped.

The easiest way to add the required settings to the `.cscfg` file is to open the `Roles` subfolder, right-click the role we want to modify, and choose **Properties**.

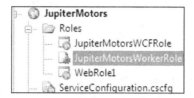

In the **Properties** panel, select the **Settings** tab, click the **Add Setting** button, and add a **String** setting. This setting will act as our `SourceSwitch` and help us determine the level of information we want to capture.

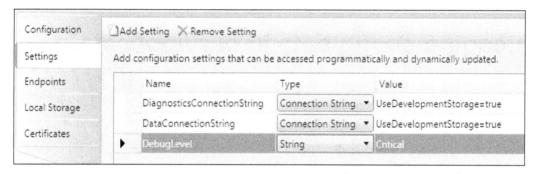

Adding a setting via the **Properties** panel makes an entry in both the `.cscfg` and the `.csdef` files. The `.csdef` file must contain a definition for every setting in the `.cscfg` file, and cannot be edited in a live application. Therefore, we cannot add additional settings to a live application, but we can change their values.

The final step is to add a few lines of code to help our application determine if it's running on IIS or Azure. We simply need to check for `RoleEnvironment.IsAvailable`, which is available only in Azure.

```
Dim _debugLevel As String
If RoleEnvironment.IsAvailable Then
    ' gets the value from .cscfg file
    _debugLevel = RoleEnvironment.GetConfigurationSettingValue(
                                            "DebugLevel")
Else
    ' gets the value from web.config file
    _debugLevel = WebConfigurationManager.AppSettings("DebugLevel")
End If
```

The template projects include configuration settings for
`DiagnosticsConnectionString` and `DataConnectionString`. By default, these
connections point to a local SQL Server Express instance on our development
machines, and obviously the connection strings need to be updated when we deploy
our application. Again, if we weren't using a default template, we'd need to add
these configuration settings too.

There are two useful resources about working with diagnostic logging and
configuration files in Azure—one is an MSDN article titled *Take Control of Logging
and Tracing in Windows Azure* (`http://msdn.microsoft.com/en-us/magazine/
ff714589.aspx`), and a code project article titled *Windows Azure Development Deep
Dive: Working With Configuration* (`http://www.codeproject.com/KB/azure/azure-
configuration.aspx`), on which part of the MSDN article is based.

Logging config data in our application

Now that we have the collection of diagnostic data configured, we need to add code
to our application to send diagnostic data to the listeners. We can do this simply by
making calls to the methods in the `System.Diagnostics.Trace` class (documented
at `http://msdn.microsoft.com/en-us/library/36hhw2t6.aspx`).

One of the more common methods we'll call is `Trace.Writeline`, as seen here:

```
Trace.Writeline("An error has occurred!","Error")
```

If our filter is set to the value `Error` or higher, our message would be logged. An
alternative, easier syntax is:

```
Trace.TraceError("An error has occurred!")
```

Again, if our filter is set to the value `Error` or higher, our message will be logged.
The simplified methods are limited to `TraceError`, `TraceInformation`, and
`TraceWarning`, whereas the `WriteLine` method can be used to log diagnostic
data at any level, including custom levels.

Transferring and persisting diagnostic
data

As diagnostic data are logged, the data are buffered in memory. In order for us to
retain the data for analysis, we need to make sure that the data persists in a proper
storage container. This is not set up by default, but it takes only a couple of lines
of code to configure the transfer of data into the storage location. We can set this
transfer to be either scheduled, or on demand.

To automatically transfer the diagnostic data on a schedule, we just need to add a single line to our role's `OnStart` method:

```
diagConfig.PerformanceCounters.ScheduledTransferPeriod = System.
TimeSpan.FromMinutes(1.0)
```

The entire `OnStart` method for our web role now reads like this:

```
Public Overrides Function OnStart() As Boolean
    Dim diagConfig As DiagnosticMonitorConfiguration =
        DiagnosticMonitor.GetDefaultInitialConfiguration()
    Dim procTimeConfig As PerformanceCounterConfiguration =
        New PerformanceCounterConfiguration()
    procTimeConfig.CounterSpecifier = "\Processor(*)\% Processor Time"
    procTimeConfig.SampleRate = System.TimeSpan.FromSeconds(1.0)
    diagConfig.PerformanceCounters.DataSources.Add(procTimeConfig)

    diagConfig.PerformanceCounters.ScheduledTransferPeriod =
        System.TimeSpan.FromMinutes(1.0)

    DiagnosticMonitor.Start("DiagnosticsConnectionString")

    Return MyBase.OnStart()
End Function
```

We'll need to add similar code to the `OnStart` methods of the other roles in our application if we want to automatically transfer the diagnostic logs for those roles too.

An on-demand transfer is a little different—an on-demand transfer can be initiated either from within the role, from another role in the same application, or even a completely different application. To reduce the amount of diagnostic data we need to sort through when debugging, we might want to log every level of diagnostic data but transfer the diagnostic data only when an error occurs.

```
Public Sub TransferDiagnosticData()

        Dim diagManager As DeploymentDiagnosticManager =
            New DeploymentDiagnosticManager(<Azure storage account
            name>, <Azure deployment ID>)

        dim roleInstDiagMgr as RoleInstanceDiagnosticManager =
            diagManager.GetRoleInstanceDiagnosticManager(
            <Role name>, <Role instance name>)

        Dim dataBuffersToTransfer As DataBufferName =
            DataBufferName.Directories
```

```
        Dim transferOptions As OnDemandTransferOptions =
            New OnDemandTransferOptions()

        With transferOptions
                .From = DateTime.MinValue
                .To = DateTime.UtcNow
        End With

        Dim requestID As Guid =
        roleInstDiagMgr.BeginOnDemandTransfer(dataBuffersToTransfer,
          transferOptions)


    End Sub
```

Complete documentation for transferring buffered data to storage can be found at http://msdn.microsoft.com/en-us/library/ee830425.aspx.

It's important to note that diagnostic data is treated the same as any other data associated with our application, and we will be charged for the storage of the diagnostic output.

Accessing stored data

Once we've transferred the diagnostic data to storage, we can access it for analysis. Accessing log data is the same as accessing any other Table or Blob Storage. The most convenient way may be using the REST interface documented earlier in this book.

As Azure becomes more popular, third-party diagnostic tools will be developed. One such tool already available is the Cerebrata Azure Diagnostics Manager, found at http://www.cerebrata.com/Products/AzureDiagnosticsManager/Default. aspx. Hundreds of Azure-related applications have been added to Codeplex as well, but many of these projects have withered.

Summary

In this chapter, we looked at the diagnostic information available to us in Azure, how to capture that information, and how to access the information once captured. Azure provides us with a familiar set of diagnostic information, which we can enable with very little work. Once enabled, we must make sure that the diagnostic data persists in either Table or Blob Storage where we can access the data as we would any other table or blob, or we can use a third-party tool designed specifically for diagnostic analysis.

15
Deploying to Windows Azure

It's the time we've been waiting for. We've successfully developed, tested, and debugged our application locally. Now all we need to do is to get it in the cloud for the others to start using! In this chapter, we'll cover:

- Configuring the Windows Azure portal with our projects and services
- Preparing our application for deployment
- Deploying our application
- Running our application post-deployment

Setting up hosted service in Windows Azure

We already have set up our project under Windows Live ID in the Windows Azure Developer portal (*Chapter 5, Introduction to SQL Azure*), but we don't have our hosted service yet. It will take only a few minutes to set it up and get it ready for our project.

The first thing to do is to log into the portal at `http://www.windows.azure.com`. Once we have logged in, we will see all of our Windows Azure projects under **My Projects** (in this case, we have only one; yet, as growth happens in the cloud, we can host multiple projects under a single Windows Live ID).

We need to click on our project name to get access to our services.

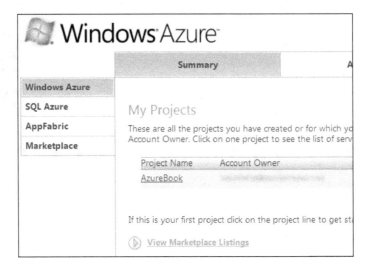

In this next screen in the portal, we see two easy links to get started on adding a new service. Click either of the circled links:

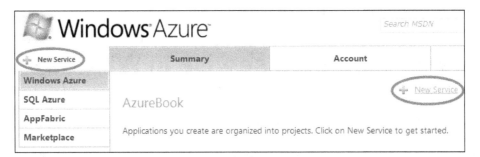

There are two different types of services for Windows Azure: **Storage Account** and **Hosted Services**. We learned about the Storage Account service when we first went over our Blob, Queue, and Table Storage, but what is this Hosted Service? It's the home for our applications (web and worker roles), configuration, and settings on the Windows Azure Fabric Controller. Choose the Hosted Services to continue our setup process.

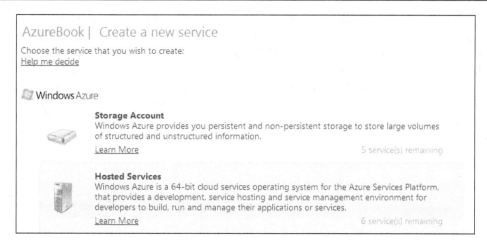

Setting Hosted Service identifiers

Once we pick the Hosted Service, it's time to configure the service. In the first step of the setup, we'll have to choose a label (name) and description for the service. These names and descriptions are just friendly identifiers for the service, and are used in the Windows Azure Developer portal, Visual Studio Publishing Wizard, and the Windows Azure Management Tool (`http://code.msdn.microsoft.com/windowsazuremmc`).

After we've put a label and description to our Hosted Service, click the **Next** button to move onto the second page of the workflow, where we'll define our **Public Service Name** for our public URL. This must be globally unique, so we must choose a name that no other Hosted Service is currently using. There is a button conveniently located next to the control that allows us to check the availability of the chosen name. As we see, the label beneath the form indicates that the name we have chosen for our public URL is available.

Public Hosted Service URL

Select a public name for your hosted service. This name must be globally unique.

Public Service Name: http:// jupitermotors   .cloudapp.net   [Check Availability]

jupitermotors is available.

Affinity Groups—geographically grouping services

Next, we'll choose an Affinity Group for our Hosted Service. Affinity Groups are a nice way to allow us to choose where our applications and services will live, and also gives us some key benefits. By creating an Affinity Group and assigning services to the group, a few things happen.

First, Windows Azure makes the best effort to put all of the assigned services into a single data center in the specified geographic region. What does this do? Well, it helps execute faster transactions between services within the same data center. There will be fewer hops in the network for communication between the services.

Another benefit to keeping your dependent services in a single affinity group is that Microsoft doesn't charge for bandwidth used within data center region. This will help keep costs lower as the services will not need to leave the data center for communication between each other, and you will not be billed for bandwidth related to the communications. However, note that transactions are still billable even when in the same data center, so it's not entirely free to communicate between services within the same data center.

One last thing to consider when choosing our Affinity Group is where the majority of our users will be. If we have a concentrated area of traffic from our customers, it's best to choose the region closest to that area. That will speed up the request and response time from and to our customers over the Internet.

For our example, imagine our customer base is mainly in the United States, primarily in the Chicago, IL area. As this area is in the central US, toward the northern end of the country, we are going to choose the North Central US region for our Affinity Group. Because we've already set up our storage account, we're going to tell Windows Azure that we have another service that is related to this Hosted Service and that we wish to create a new Affinity Group. Our Affinity Group will be descriptively named **North Central United States**. Click the **Create** button, and we're all finished for now.

Preparation application for deployment

Because we've been using our configuration files for our connection strings in the cloud project, we need to make a few small changes. Let's change the connection strings in our configuration files in Visual Studio.

In our cloud project, for each role in our `Roles` folder, we need to perform the following steps:

1. Right-click the role and choose **Properties**.

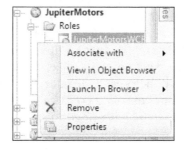

2. Choose the **Settings** tab, and you should see our connection strings pointing to our Development Storage.

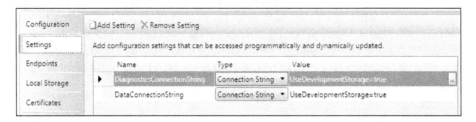

3. These connection strings will be required to change to point to our Storage Account in the cloud. This can be easily done by clicking the "**...**" button to the far right of the connection string. It's going to ask us for some information such as the account name and the account key, both of which were provided when setting up the Storage Account. We can look these up in the Windows Azure Developer portal if we cannot remember them.

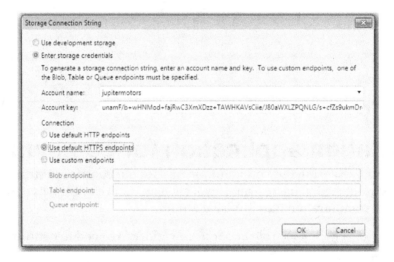

4. Finally, the last step is to publish the cloud project. We can easily do this by right-clicking on the cloud project and choosing **Publish...**. We will get a window once again, asking us how we want to publish our cloud project. We have an option of creating the Service Package only, or deploying directly to Windows Azure. Because we love working in the Windows Azure Developer portal, we're just going to select the **Create the Service Package Only** option, which will help package everything up into two files—one is .cspkg file, which is our compiled code for our cloud project roles, and the other is the .cscfg file, which is our configuration settings file for our cloud project roles.

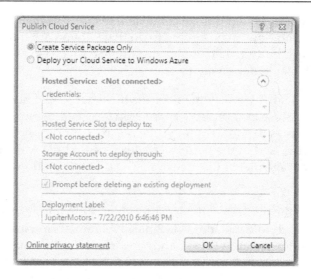

Ready for deployment

It's time to play in the Windows Azure Developer portal once again. We're going to give it all the information needed to get our cloud project up and running in Windows Azure.

Let's go to our Hosted Service and see what we have there.

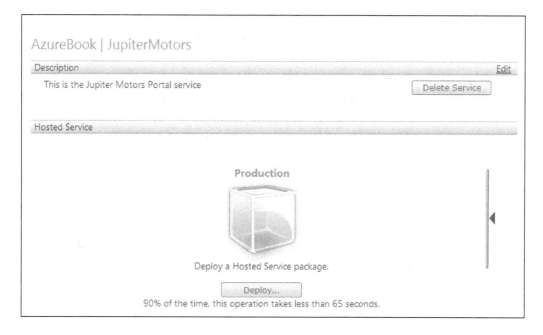

This looks nice and easy. What did we come here to do? The answer is to deploy our cloud project. And how are we going to do that? If you are thinking we should click on the **Deploy**... button, then you're absolutely correct. Go ahead and click the **Deploy...** button to begin deployment.

The next step is also fairly easy. Remember the files that Visual Studio created for us when we published the cloud project? We're going to need them here. Both files were created in the solution's `Bin` folder, under the release configuration named folder (Debug, Release, etc.), and in the `Publish` folder. The first file we're looking for is the Application Package file, or the .cspkg file. The Configuration Settings file is the .cscfg file.

The next section on the deployment page asks about Operating System Settings. What's this? Well, each role instance is technically a miniature virtual machine running in the Windows Azure Fabric, and the virtual machine needs an OS. The OS builds are a miniature version of Windows Server 2008 (limited feature set). This OS is constantly worked on to patch any security flaws, fix bugs, and all the other typical everyday maintenance you would expect a company to do to maintain a server OS. There are options on which OS version we would like our applications to run against if we choose the Manual OS Upgrade Method. Here's the catch: Depending on which SDK we built our application with, we need to choose a compatible OS to use. To choose the correct OS, click the **What are the Options?** link and the article maintained by Microsoft will let you know the minimum OS that can be used. All SDKs are supported by the newer operating systems.

Because the newest OS version supports our SDK, we're going to let Windows Azure automatically upgrade our OS and choose the newest OS for us at time of deployment.

Finally, we need to name (label) our deployment. This is just to help us know about this deployment. We could use a release or version number, a timestamp, among other things, to help us know what is deployed.

Once these steps are all completed, click the **Deploy** button and let Windows Azure do some magic!

The Windows Azure Developer portal will keep us updated on the progress of the deployment.

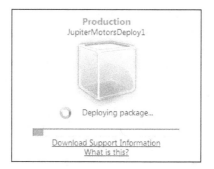

Congratulations! Our cloud project is deployed! Are we done? Well, the answer is not at all. It's in the cloud, but it's not doing anything yet. We'll get to that in a little while, but first, let's have a quick look at changing the configuration in the portal.

Changing live configuration

We don't need to change the configuration in Visual Studio and redeploy our cloud package just to make configuration setting changes. We're provided with a nice text editor in the portal to make changes on the fly. Assume our connection string needs to be changed, we can do that. Need more instances of a role, we can manage that as well!

To do this, go to our Hosted Service page and click the **Configure...** button below our deployed package (cube).

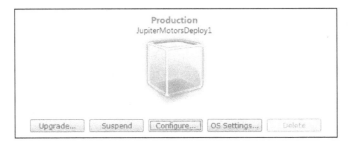

The page with the text editor will be displayed. We can make our changes right in this textbox if we want. We can also upload a new configuration file from our Visual Studio build. Make the necessary changes or browse to the new file and click the **Upload** button. Once the changes have been made manually or the new file has been uploaded, click the **Save** button.

Upgrading the deployment

We have an option to upgrade our deployment on the fly in the portal. At our Hosted Service page, all we need to do is click the **Upgrade...** button. A quick note for us to remember: we can upgrade a deployment as long as service model is identical. In other words, we cannot upgrade if we added or deleted a role to our cloud project.

We will be asked a lot of the same information as the initial deployment (Application Package file, Configuration Settings file, Operating System Settings, and Deployment Name) but we do have two new options: **Upgrade Mode** and **Service Upgrade**.

For the Upgrade Mode, we can choose whether we want Windows Azure to upgrade our upgrade domains in sequence, or if we want to upgrade manually. Wait a second! We first need to understand what an upgrade domain. **Upgrade domains** are logical groupings of running instances. There are two upgrade domains by default. For example, imagine we had one role, with 10 different instances of it running. Now that there are two upgrade domains, each one would have five instances. With this upgrade mode, we could have Windows Azure automatically upgrade the first five instances in the first upgrade domain, followed by the next five instances in the other upgrade domain, or we could do it ourselves (maybe we want to upgrade the second upgrade domain first, then upgrade the first one).

The next part of the upgrade process that we haven't yet seen is the **Service Upgrade**. What's this? With service upgrade, we can update only one role in the cloud project. Consider this example. We find out one of our roles has a bug in it and we fix it. Do we really need to upgrade everything? No, we don't have to tinker with anything else. What's the first rule we should always follow? Never touch anything more than we need, especially if it's running perfectly as it is. This allows us to do just that!

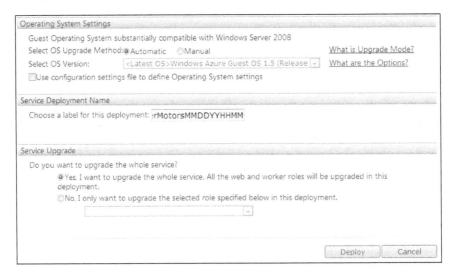

Once you have finished filling out all of these options and information, just click the **Deploy** button.

Running the deployment

It's the time that we all have been waiting for! We've deployed, changed configuration, and upgraded the deployment. Now it's time to get it running!

On our Hosted Service page, all we need to do it click the **Run** button to get things underway.

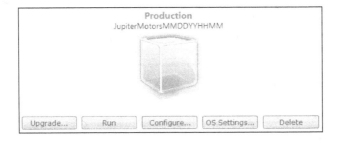

Once again, during the process when the deployment is started, the portal will give us updates along the way. Once you see the green checkmarks alongside each of our roles, we know it's all done and running!

At this point, we should be able to go to the URL below our deployment and see our application in action! It should act identical to our application in our development fabric as long as we choose a compatible OS to run our service on!

Summary

In this chapter, we set up our service in the Windows Azure Developer portal, prepared our cloud application in Visual Studio for deployment, and manually deployed our application. To examine Azure's elasticity, we changed the configuration file, and started our application in the Windows Azure cloud!

Conclusion

We've now reached the end of our exploration of Microsoft's Azure platform. Together, we've built a simple application making use of many of the features of Azure. We've explored Azure's Compute and Storage services, SQL Azure, Access Control, and Service Bus, and we've seen how our existing skills in .NET and SQL Server can be leveraged on Azure. We have tried to provide a sufficient overview of all the technologies, but some of these topics deserve entire books dedicated to them.

We hope you've found the information useful, and you now have a better understanding of the advantages and challenges presented when developing for Azure. We are positive that you can now confidently guide the technologies in your enterprise onto the platform that best serves your business needs and architectures best. Whether you choose Azure, on-premises, a mix of the two, or some other platform completely, our goal was to help you make the choice best suited for your enterprise.

Microsoft considers Azure to be its future, forming the basis for many of its service offerings, as well as providing the platform to other enterprises. Microsoft is committed to developing Azure, and there will undoubtedly be an updated version of this book in the future. There is a wealth of Azure content produced on a daily basis, found on blogs, Twitter, forums, and the Azure mini-site. The Windows Azure and SQL Azure teams blog at `http://blogs.msdn.com/b/windowsazure/` and `http://blogs.msdn.com/b/sqlazure/`, and these are the best places to follow information about the platforms.

Index

Symbols

.NET Services. *See* App Fabric

A

Access Control
  authentication, versus authorization 180
  configuration basics 181
  configuring, for Jupiter Motors 183
  overview 178, 179
  requests 182
  Sign in with Twitter button 178
  SWT 182
Access Control configuration, for Jupiter Motors
  about 183
  adding, to web service 194
  AddOrderStatusUpdateToQueue function 183
  Azure AppFabric Portal, configuring 184, 185
  client application, configuring 191
  configuration tools 186-188
  configuration tools, ACM.exe 186
  configuration tools, AcmBrowser 186
  GetStatusForOrder function 183
  Issuer, configuring 190
  LoadStartupData function 183
  Rules, configuring 190
  scope, configuring 190
  Token Policy, creating 188, 189
ACM.EXE tool 181
ACMBROWSE 181
AddOrderStatusUpdateToQueue service function 153

ALTER DATABASE command 46
Amazon
  cloud offering 12
  Virtual Private Cloud 12
AppFabric
  about 21
  using 21
application deployment
  preparing 213-215
application diagnostics
  about 123-125
  blob storage 125
  table storage 125
ASP.NET
  assembly references 120
ASP.NET developer
  considerations 22
Azure
  about 12-16
  application, diagram 38
  Azure Fabric 15
  Development Fabric 22
  features 37, 38
  monthly service charges, calculating 23
  Table Storage 93
  web role 119
Azure, developing
  local machine, configuring 27-31
  SDK, installing 31-33
  tools, downloading 27
  tools, installing 31
Azure account, creating
  about 39
  steps 39, 40
  Table Storage, adding 96

Azure AppFabric
about 177
examples 178
Service Bus service 177
Azure costs, calculating
AppFabric pricing, calculating 24
SQL Azure pricing, calculating 24
Windows Azure pricing, calculating 23, 24
Azure Diagnostics
collected data, storing 200-202
Azure ecosystem
blobs 77
Azure menu
App Fabric 16
SQL Azure 16
Windows Azure 16

B

BIDS 61
binary large object. *See* **blob**
BizTalk Services. *See* **App Fabric**
blob
about 18, 77
Create Blob parameter 88
Delete Blob parameter 89
Get Blob Metadata parameter 89
Get Blob parameter 88
Get Blob Properties parameter 89
Lease Blob parameter 90
List Blobs parameter 88
Set Blob Metadata parameter 89
Set Blob Properties parameter 89
BlobRequest.GetBlockList method 91
BlobRequest class 88
blobs, Azure ecosystem
block blobs 77
page blobs 77, 78
storage, creating 78
storing 78
Blob storage
accessing, mechanisms 83
API 84
blobs, working with 88
containers working with, REST Interface
    used 85

containers working with, StorageClient
    library used 85-87
creating, steps 78-82
REST 84
Blob Storage API
DELETE command 84
GET command 84
HEAD command 84
PUT command 84
using 84
Blob Storage Data Model
about 83
blob 83
blocks 83
container 83
built-in functions, SQL Server
Aggregate 49
Configuration 49
Cursor 49
Date and Time 49
Mathematical 49
Metadata 49
ODBC Date/Time 50
ODBC Numeric 50
ODBC String 50
Ranking 49
Security 49
String 50
System 50
Text/Image 50
Business Intelligence Development Studio.
    See **BIDS**

C

CDN 36
CDN, Windows Azure
about 82
blobs, accessing 82
blobs, caching 83
class functions
CreateDataSetFromDataReader 153
GetOrdersNotComplete 153
GetOrderStatuses 153
Clear() method 116
**client application configuration, for Access
    Control**
steps 191

Token, requesting for 192, 193
CloudBlob.CreateSnapshot method 90
CloudBlob.SetMetadata method 89
CloudBlob.UploadFile method 88
CloudBlob class 88
CloudBlobClient class 85
CloudBlobContainer.Delete method 87
CloudBlobContainer.FetchAttributes method 86
CloudBlobContainer.ListBlobs method 88
CloudBlobContainer.SetMetadata method 86
CloudBlobContainer.SetPermissions method 87
CloudBlobContainer class 85
cloud computing
   about 7-9, 13
   benefits 9
   downsides 10
   infrastructure 11, 12
cloud computing, benefits
   disaster recovery 9, 10
   familiar environment 10
   low up-front cost 9
   simplified migration 10
   storage management 9, 10
cloud computing, downsides
   higher cost 11
   hosting problem 11
   lesser control on application environment 10, 11
CloudQueue class 113
CLR 24
common language runtime. See CLR
config data
   logging, in application 206
content delivery network. See CDN
CREATE DATABASE command 65
CREATE LOGIN command 65
Create method 113
CreateTable(<tablename>) method 98

D

DAC Pack 61
data-tier application package. See DAC Pack
database
   creating 65-75

database tables
   versus Table Storage 93-95
Data Control Language. See DCL
Data Definition Language. See DDL
Data Manipulation Language. See DML
data migration, SQL Azure. See schema migration, SQL Azure
DataTables, packaging
   advantages 156
   disadvantages 156
dbmanager, SQL Azure 56
DCL 48
DDL 48
Delete method 113
DeleteObject method 102
DELETE operator 89
DeleteTableIfExist method 99
deployment
   running 220, 221
   upgrading 219, 220
development considerations
   about 54
   maximum size, managing 54
Development Fabric 22
diagnostic data
   persisting 206-208
   transferring 206-208
DiagnosticDataBufferConfiguration class 200
diagnostic logging
   configuration location, changing 204-206
   enabling 202-204
DML 48
DoesTableExist method 98

E

End User License Agreement. See EULA
enterprise application 7, 8
Enterprise Resource Planning. See ERP
entities, Table Storage
   deleting 102
   Entity Group Transactions, rules 103
   inserting 100
   merging 101
   naming rules 102
   property value, types 102

querying 100
updating 101
working with 99
ERP 35
ERPService.svc.vb, WCF web service
about 151
AddOrderStatusUpdateToQueue service
function 153
CreateDataSetFromDataReader function
153-155
GetOrdersNotComplete function 153-155
GetOrderStatuses function 153-155
GetOrderStatusForOrder service function
152
LoadStartUpData service function 152
ETW 200
EULA 31
Event Tracing for Windows. *See* **ETW**
exception handling
about 104
concurrency conflicts 105
operation, retrying 104
response codes 105
retry 105
table errors 105

F

fully supported T-SQL commands
DCL 48
DDL 48
DML 48

G

GAC 97
Generate Script Wizard. *See* **GSW**
GET/HEAD operator 86, 89
GetAll command, acm.exe 188
Get command, acm.exe 188
GetMessage() method 115
GET operator 91
GetOrderStatusForOrder service function
152
Global Assembly Cache. *See* **GAC**
Google
cloud offering 12

Google Query Language. *See* **GQL**
GQL 12
GSW 58

H

Hello Fabric sample 202
hosted service setup, Windows Azure
about 209, 210
Affinity Group, choosing 212, 213
Identifiers, setting up 211, 212
Huron 20

I

identity providers 179
IERPService.vb file, WCF web service
about 149
ADO.NET datasets, using 151
Data Contract 150
Operation Contract 150
Service Contract 150
include=metadata parameter 111

J

Jupiter ERP database
SQL Azure portal 64, 65
visual look 62, 63
JupiterMotorsERP local application
about 170-172
App.config code, adding 173, 174
designing, requirements 171
Jupiter Motors Web Role
about 126, 127
additional stored procedures 128-142
code 128
portal page, viewing 126, 127
Jupiter Motors web service 145
Jupiter Motors worker role
about 163
building 163-168

K

key
Current Management Key 184
Previous Management Key 184

L

ListQueues method 112
ListTables method 98
live configuration
  changing 218
LoadStartUpData service function 152
local machine configuration
  Microsoft Hotfixes, applying 30
  registry tool, using 28
  steps 27-29
  WCF HTTP Activation, enabling 30
loginmanager, SQL Azure 56

M

management tools
  about 55
  Access 2010 56
  Project Houston 55, 56
  SQL Azure portal 55
  SSMS 2008 R2 55
marker parameter 111
MARS 50
maxresults parameter 111
MERGE method 101
messages, working with
  about 114
  Delete messages parameter 116
  Get messages parameter 115
  Peek messages parameter 116
  Put messages parameter 115
metadata, queues
  adding, REST API used 113
  in client library 114
  retrieving 114
  setting 113
method
  BlobRequest.GetBlockList 91
  CloudBlob.CreateSnapshot 90
  CloudBlob.SetMetadata 89
  CloudBlob.UploadFile 88
  CloudBlobContainer.Delete 87
  CloudBlobContainer.FetchAttributes 86
  CloudBlobContainer.ListBlobs 88
  CloudBlobContainer.SetMetadata 86
  CloudBlobContainer.SetPermissions 87
  Create 113

CreateTable(<tablename>) 98
  Delete 113
  ListTables 98
  methodTokenValidator.Validate 195
  OnStart() 159
  OnStop() 160
  Run() 159
  SetMetadata 114
Microsoft Azure. *See* Azure
Microsoft Online Services Customer Portal.
    See MOCP
MOCP 40
multiple active result sets. *See* MARS

O

Object-Relational Mapping. *See* ORM
OnStart() method 159, 202, 207
OnStop() method 160
ORM 95

P

partially supported T-SQL commands
  Create/Alter/Drop Index 49
  Create/Alter/Drop Table 49
  Create/Alter/Drop Trigger 49
  Create/Alter Function 49
  Create/Alter View 49
PartitionKey
  choosing 103
  choosing, Microsoft tips 104
prefix parameter 111
Project Dallas 22
project design
  about 35
  Azure selection, need for 36
  customer portal, components 36
  information flow, overview 36
Project Houston, management tools
  about 55
  advantage 56
PUT operator 91

Q

querystring parameters
  numofmessages 115

visibilitytimeout 115
queues
creating 112
deleting 113
listing 111
metadata, obtaining 114
metadata, setting 113
working with 111
queues, creating
in client library 113
REST API 112, 113
rules 112
queues, deleting
client library, using 113
REST API 113
queues, listing
Client library 112
REST API 111
Queue Storage
about 107, 108
accessing 108
benefits 109
binary data, handling 110
failover 109
invisibility time 110

R

recreational vehicles. *See* **RVs**
regedit command 28
Representational State Transfer. *See* **REST**
REST 84
Role.OnStart() method 203
Run() method 159
RVs 35

S

SaveChanges method 101, 103
schema migration, SQL Azure
about 57
BCP 62
data, scripting manually 57, 58
objects, scripting manually 57, 58
SQL Azure Migration Wizard 58, 59
SSIS 59
security, SQL Azure
about 53, 54

rules 53
security token service. *See* **STS**
Service Bus
about 195
as connection broker 197
as message relay 196
as message relay, advantages 196
as message relay, disadvantages 197
service function
AddOrderStatusUpdateToQueue 152
LoadStartUpData 152
Service Policy 181
SetMetadata method 114
Simple Web Token. *See* **SWT**
SQL Azure
about 20
benefits 42
data, migrating 57
databases, managing 56
dbmanager 56
differences 50
loginmanager 56
logins, managing 56
overview 41, 42
pricing, calculating 24
roles, managing 56
schema, migrating 57
security 53
similarities 47
SQL Azure, benefits
familiar development model 46, 47
high availability 42, 45
manageability 42
Relational data model 46
scalability 42, 46
SQL Azure, differences
about 50
database number 51
database objects 51
data synchronization 52, 53
Distributed Transaction Coordinator (DTC) 51
Service Broker 51
SQL Browser 51
system functions 52
T-SQL commands 51, 52

SQL Azure, managing
about 43
differences 44, 45
high availability 45
similarities 43, 44
steps 43
SQL Azure, similarities
built-in functions 49, 50
database objects 47
fully supported T-SQL commands 48
multiple active result sets 50
partially supported T-SQL commands 49
T-SQL commands support 48
SQL Azure Manager 20
SQL Server Analysis Services. *See* **SSAS**
SQL Server Integration Services. *See* **SSIS**
SQL Server Management Studio. *See* **SSMS**
SQL Server Reporting Services. *See* **SSRS**
SSAS 41
SSIS
about 59
DAC Packages 61, 62
packages, creating from scratch 61
SQL Server Import and Export Wizard
59-61
SSMS 20
SSRS 41
storage service, Windows Azure
about 18
Blob Storage 19
Queue Storage 19
Table Storage 19
stored data
accessing 208
STS 179
SWT 182
System.Diagnostics.Trace class 206
System.Net.Sockets.TcpListener class 161

T

tables, Table Storage
creating 98
deleting 99
list, querying 98
naming convention 98
working with 98

Table Storage
accessing 97
adding to Azure account 96
benefits 95
entities, working with 99
limitations 96
tables, accessing 95, 96
use 94
versus database tables 93-95
Table Storage, accessing
about 97
tables, naming convention 98
tables, working with 98
x-ms-version property 97
time-to-live. *See* **TTL**
Token Policy 181
TokenValidator.Validate method 195
TokenValidator class 194
trace listener 124
TTL 83

U

UpdateObject method 101
Upgrade domains 219

V

visual representation, container 83

W

Warehouse Management System. *See* **WMS**
WCF
about 144
new Web Role, creating 145-149
securing 144
WCF web service
about 149
ERPService.svc.vb 151
IERPService.vb file 149
web role
about 119
and ASP.NET 120
Jupiter Motors Web Role 126, 127
project, creating 121-123
solution, creating 121-123

web service
adding, to Azure Web Role 144
endpoint 143
endpoint, components 143
host environment 143
Jupiter Motors web service 145
service class 143
Web Service Definition Language. *See*
    WSDL
Windows application
listboxes, populating 169
overview 169
testing 175, 176
Windows Azure. *See* **also Azure**
Windows Azure
about 17
AppFabric 21
Azure Fabric Agent 20
Azure Fabric controller 20
CDN 82
cloud project, running 215-217
compute service 17
developing 27
Fabric Controller 17
hosted service, setting up 209, 210
pricing, calculating 23
Queue Storage 107
Service Bus 13

storage service 17, 18
Windows Azure tools, installing
Platform Training Kit, installing 31
SDK, installing 32
steps 33
tools, installing 32
Windows Communication Foundation. *See*
    WCF
Windows Live ID. *See* **WLID**
WLID 39
WMS 21
WorkerRole class 165
worker roles
about 159
best practices 162
building 159, 160
facing externally 161
Jupiter Motors worker role 163
managing 161, 162
thread-pool pattern 161
uses 160
WriteLine method 206
WSDL 156, 157

X

x-ms-version, Table Storage 97

Thank you for buying
Microsoft Azure: Enterprise Application Development

About Packt Publishing

Packt, pronounced 'packed', published its first book "Mastering phpMyAdmin for Effective MySQL Management" in April 2004 and subsequently continued to specialize in publishing highly focused books on specific technologies and solutions.

Our books and publications share the experiences of your fellow IT professionals in adapting and customizing today's systems, applications, and frameworks. Our solution based books give you the knowledge and power to customize the software and technologies you're using to get the job done. Packt books are more specific and less general than the IT books you have seen in the past. Our unique business model allows us to bring you more focused information, giving you more of what you need to know, and less of what you don't.

Packt is a modern, yet unique publishing company, which focuses on producing quality, cutting-edge books for communities of developers, administrators, and newbies alike. For more information, please visit our website: www.packtpub.com.

About Packt Enterprise

In 2010, Packt launched two new brands, Packt Enterprise and Packt Open Source, in order to continue its focus on specialization. This book is part of the Packt Enterprise brand, home to books published on enterprise software – software created by major vendors, including (but not limited to) IBM, Microsoft and Oracle, often for use in other corporations. Its titles will offer information relevant to a range of users of this software, including administrators, developers, architects, and end users.

Writing for Packt

We welcome all inquiries from people who are interested in authoring. Book proposals should be sent to author@packtpub.com. If your book idea is still at an early stage and you would like to discuss it first before writing a formal book proposal, contact us; one of our commissioning editors will get in touch with you.

We're not just looking for published authors; if you have strong technical skills but no writing experience, our experienced editors can help you develop a writing career, or simply get some additional reward for your expertise.

Refactoring with Microsoft Visual Studio 2010

ISBN: 978-1-849680-10-3   Paperback: 372 pages

Evolve your software system to support new and ever-changing requirements by updating your C# code base with patterns and principles

1. Make your code base maintainable with refactoring

2. Support new features more easily by making your system adaptable

3. Enhance your system with an improved object-oriented design and increased encapsulation and componentization

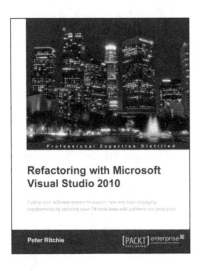

Expert Cube Development with Microsoft SQL Server 2008 Analysis Services

ISBN: 978-1-847197-22-1   Paperback: 360 pages

Design and implement fast, scalable and maintainable cubes

1. A real-world guide to designing cubes with Analysis Services 2008

2. Model dimensions and measure groups in BI Development Studio

3. Implement security, drill-through, and MDX calculations

4. Learn how to deploy, monitor, and performance-tune your cube

Please check **www.PacktPub.com** for information on our titles

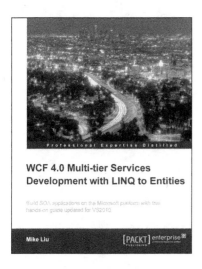
WCF 4.0 Multi-tier Services Development with LINQ to Entities

ISBN: 978-1-849681-14-8   Paperback: 348 pages

Build SOA applications on the Microsoft platform
with this hands-on guide updated for VS2010

1. Master WCF and LINQ to Entities concepts by
    completing practical examples and applying
    them to your real-world assignments

2. The first and only book to combine WCF and
    LINQ to Entities in a multi-tier real-world
    WCF service

3. Ideal for beginners who want to build scalable,
    powerful, easy-to-maintain WCF services

.NET Compact Framework 3.5 Data Driven Applications

ISBN: 978-1-849690-10-2   Paperback: 484 pages

Build robust and feature-rich mobile data-driven
applications with the help of real-world examples

1. Develop data-driven mobile applications from
    the ground up on top of the Oracle Lite and
    SQL Server Lite databases

2. Build ergonomic User Interfaces targeting the
    mobile platform that you can easily adapt for
    your business applications

3. Optimize performance and security on the
    mobile platform as well as drawing useful
    charts and reports using .NET CF's graphics
    libraries for your data-driven applications

Please check **www.PacktPub.com** for information on our titles